Wild Wellington *Ngā Taonga Taiao*

WILD WELLINGTON

NGĀ TAONGA TAIAO

A guide to the wildlife
and wild places
of Te Upoko-o-te-Ika

MICHAEL SZABO

KARAKIA

Ka huri taku aro ki Turakirae. Ka mau te wehi,
ā, ko ahau ko koe – ko koe ko ahau.

Ka piki ake rā ki Remutaka. Ka mau te wehi,
ā, ko ahau ko koe – ko koe ko ahau.

Ka nuku, ka neke ki Pipinui. Ka mau te wehi,
ā, ko ahau ko koe – ko koe ko ahau.

Ka tau, ka rarau ki Rimurapa. Ka mau te wehi,
ā, ko ahau ko koe – ko koe ko ahau.

Tēnei ahau, tēnei ahau. Tēnei te amokura nā
Tokomaru, he kāwai nō runga i te rangi.

As I gaze upon Turakirae, I am filled with awe,
for I am you – and you are me.

As I climb the ranges to Remutaka, I am filled
with awe, for I am you – and you are me.

As I journey to Pipinui, I am filled with awe,
for I am you – and you are me.

As I find solace in Rimurapa, I am filled with
awe, for I am you – and you are me.

I am a product of the places above, the
spaces below, and everything in between.
I am a descendant of the waka Tokomaru,
a child of the heavens.

Neavin Broughton (Te Āti Awa, Taranaki Tūturu, Ngā Iwi o Taranaki ki te Tonga), 2024

TE ŌHĀKĪ A TE WHAREPŌURI

I muri nei kia pai ki aku taonga Māori, taonga Pākehā, kia tae ake te haruru o te reo ki ahau i Te Rēinga.

After I have gone be good to my Māori people and my European people, let the thunder of your voice reach me in the spirit land.

The only known portrait of Te Wharepōuri. One half of Plate I from *Illustrations to 'Adventure in New Zealand'* by Edward Jerningham Wakefield (London: Smith, Elder and Company, 1845). Lithograph by Day and Haghe. Alexander Turnbull Library, Ref: PUBL-0011-02-1

CONTENTS

Introduction   9

PŌNEKE WELLINGTON CITY

He oranga wai, he oranga tangata: As waterways thrive, so too do people   21

1. Zealandia Te Māra a Tāne   24
2. Ōtari–Wilton's Bush Reserve   34
3. Wellington Botanic Garden Ki Paekākā   44
4. Te Ahumairangi   52
5. Mount Tarikākā and Khandallah Park loop track   58
6. Pōneke Wellington waterfront   64
7. Matairangi Mount Victoria   72
8. Waimapihi Reserve   78

PŌNEKE KI TE TONGA THE SOUTH COAST

Ngā tai karekare o te tonga: The turbulent seas of the southern coast   86

9. Oruaiti Reserve and Breaker Bay   90
10. Rangitatau Palmer Head and Tarakena Bay   94
11. Taputeranga Marine Reserve and coast   98
12. Te Kopahou Reserve including Spooky Gully   108
13. Te Haape Stream valley   116
14. Pariwhero Red Rocks Scientific Reserve and Te Rimurapa Sinclair Head   122
15. Te Moana-o-Raukawa Cook Strait ferry   128
16. Nicholson Canyon and Cook Canyon pelagic seabirds   132

TE AWA KAIRANGI THE HUTT VALLEY

Te mākurukuru o Te Awa Kairangi: The profuse abundance of the Hutt Valley — 142

17. Korokoro Dam Loop Track, in Belmont Regional Park — 146
18. Pito One Beach and Te Awa Kairangi Hutt River mouth — 152
19. Matiu Somes Island scientific and historic reserve — 158
20. East Harbour Regional Park northern forest including Ōtuamotoro, Muritai and Butterfly Creek — 164
21. Parangarahu Lakes at Te Rae-akiaki — 186
22. Puketahā forest in Wainuiomata Mainland Island — 192
23. Percy Scenic Reserve and alpine plant collection — 200
24. Kaitoke Regional Park swingbridge track circuit — 206

MAI TE AWARUA-O-PORIRUA KI ŌTAIHANGA PORIRUA AND KAPITI COAST

He whānau, he whenua: Connecting whānau with whenua — 215

25. Pāuatahanui Wildlife Reserve — 218
26. Plimmerton Beach and foreshore — 224
27. Mana Island Scientific Reserve — 230
28. Kapiti Island Nature Reserve — 236
29. Kapiti Marine Reserve — 242
30. Waikanae Estuary Scientific Reserve — 246

More wild places — 254
Glossary — 256
Acknowledgements — 258
About the author and photographer — 260
Image credits — 261
Index — 262

INTRODUCTION

Have you ever seen a kekeno New Zealand fur seal basking on a rock, a flock of kākā flying overhead, or a kiwi walking through a tangle of ferns? You can find all of these and more in the 'natural capital' of Aotearoa New Zealand: Wild Wellington.

You can see kākā and tūī in city parks, kororā little blue penguins and whai keo eagle rays swimming in the harbour, and kiwi during night tours of the world's first fully fenced urban ecosanctuary, Zealandia Te Māra a Tāne in Karori. But what about the kōkako, weka, hihi stitchbird, tītitipounamu rifleman and kārearea New Zealand falcon? Or giant wētā, rāpoka leopard seals, geckos or manaia seahorses? This guide will show you where, when and how to look for them – and, hopefully, improve your chances of seeing them.

There are so many ways to appreciate nature here, from walking in wild places, bird and wildlife watching, botanising and photography, to swimming, snorkelling, scuba diving and kayaking. The amazing diversity that occurs here ranges from elegant pūrerehua butterflies to majestic toroa albatrosses, sleek aihe common dolphins to maki orca mega-dolphins, delicate native orchids to giant rimu, and tiny filmy ferns to towering tree ferns.

Wild Wellington has many of the geographical features that typify Aotearoa. From the maunga at Puketahā in Wainuiomata, 767 metres above sea level, down to the depths of Cook Canyon at 600 metres below sea level, there are ngahere forests, repo wetlands, awa rivers, roto lakes, pūwaha estuaries, motu islands, sandy takutai beaches, and underwater toka rocky reefs.

This guide covers the wider Te Upoko-o-te Ika metropolitan area, which comprises about 2250 square kilometres when Pōneke is combined with Porirua, the Hutt Valley, Wainuiomata and the Kapiti Coast, and includes hundreds of publicly owned parks, reserves and beaches, many with scenic landscapes and breathtaking views.

The wild places included here are all connected by the birds that move between them and the complex food webs they help to sustain. Wild Wellington is also connected to the rest of Aotearoa, Polynesia, Melanesia, Antarctica and Arctic Alaska through the migratory movements of the marine mammals, seabirds, wading birds and fishes that live here or visit for part of the year.

Each chapter showcases what you can see at each site through the passing year. At the Zealandia ecosanctuary, for instance, the focus is on the native birds and tuatara, at Taputeranga Marine Reserve the wealth of coastal marine wildlife, and at East Harbour Regional Park the tawhai beech forest and native orchids. At Ōtari–Wilton's Bush it shifts to the old-growth podocarp forest and native flowering plants, at the Parangarahu Lakes to the wetland birds and coastal plants, at Waikanae estuary to the nesting tara terns and freshwater ika fish, and at Kapiti Island to the haunting calls of kōkako and kiwi.

The chapters also describe some impressive wildlife spectacles, from the kekeno New Zealand fur seal winter haul-out at Te Rimurapa Sinclair Head and pods of aihe common dolphins and maki orca that visit coastal waters and the harbour, to the raucous flocks of kākā and tūī that flock to feed on spring-flowering kōwhai and winter-flowering kohekohe in the Botanic Garden and other city parks.

You can also see the world's largest flying seabirds – toroa albatrosses – flying off the south coast and over Cook Strait, bustling tara tern and kawau shag colonies on the coast, and in summer the whai keo eagle rays and koinga rig houndsharks that swim in the shallows off Oriental Bay and in Whairepo Lagoon.

There are spectacular crimson-flowering northern rātā forests and colourful coteries of fragrant native orchids, and tranquillity can be found among the verdant ferns growing under the native forest giants that tower over Ōtuamotoro Days Bay, Kaitoke and Puketahā.

There is also tawhai beech 'goblin' forest to explore near Wainuiomata, and an eye-catching community of upland plant species to discover in the steep hill country on the south coast including taramea speargrass, īnanga needle-leaf grass-tree, and cushion plant relatives of 'vegetable sheep'.

Together, the sites covered in this guide offer a representative selection of publicly accessible wild places in the wider Te Upoko-o-te-Ika area. The extensive public transport system means you can reach them by bus or train, or in a few cases by ferry, cable car or EV shuttle bus. They can all be explored on foot, and some have wheelchair access. Details of how to access the sites are provided in each chapter.

So there is something here for everyone, from short walks in urban parks to longer hikes up and down maunga, and from short ferry rides to an all-day pelagic seabird-watching trip at sea.

A UNIQUE COMMUNITY OF SPECIES

Over 80 percent of all New Zealand bird species are native to Aotearoa, and about 45 percent of the total are endemic species that only breed in Aotearoa. This guide covers the native and endemic species; it does not focus on introduced species except to mention invasive pests.

The 'natural capital' of Aotearoa is significant in having such a wide range of endemic bird species that breed in its wild places. Here in wild Wellington, these include kiwi pukupuku little spotted kiwi, kārearea New Zealand falcon, tītitipounamu rifleman, hihi stitchbird, tīeke saddleback, kākā, kākāriki, pōpokotea whitehead, pāteke brown teal, toutouwai North Island robin, korimako bellbird, tūī and kawau tikitiki spotted shag.

Three kiwi species breed in the wider Te Upoko-o-te-Ika area, at Kapiti and Mana Island, Zealandia and Puketahā forest (kiwi pukupuku little spotted, kiwi-nui North Island brown, rowi Ōkarito brown), which is more kiwi species than in any other metropolitan area of the country.

Some endemic species, such as tītitipounamu rifleman, tuatara, Te Hoiere pepeketua Maud Island frog, kapokapowai bush giant dragonfly and the carnivorous giant land snails, have been described as the 'ghosts of Gondwana' because they are thought to be survivors of ancient lineages that date from the time before Aotearoa broke away from the Gondwana supercontinent 80 million years ago. All of them breed in wild Wellington.

The three largest offshore islands are important havens for threatened birds: Kapiti for kiwi pukupuku, weka, kōkako, koekoeā long-tailed cuckoo, hihi stitchbird and tīeke saddleback; Mana for takahē, mātātā fernbird and rowi Ōkarito brown kiwi; and Matiu for red-crowned kākāriki, kawau tikitiki spotted shag and kororā little blue penguin. Mana is also the global stronghold of the Cook Strait giant wētā, McGregor's skink and moko mangaeka goldstripe gecko.

Mainland Te Upoko-o-te-Ika is a stronghold for breeding seabirds. These include kawau shags (five species), tara tern (one species) and gull (two species), plus kororā little blue penguins. Five more species – tītī sooty shearwater, pakahā fluttering shearwater, tītī wainui fairy prion, kuaka common diving petrel and takahikare white-faced storm petrel – nest on four of the offshore islands (Kapiti, Mana, Matiu Somes, Mākaro Ward). There are also dozens of other native species, including forest birds, wading birds and wetland birds, that can be observed at the wild places described here.

MAKING THE MOST OF YOUR TIME

Binoculars can help you make the most of your time at these sites by giving you better views of native wildlife, and a smartphone can be useful for taking close-up photos that you can later enlarge on a screen to view and identify smaller subjects, like some flowers or butterflies.

There are now some very informative nature-related Facebook groups that are free to use and can help you connect with nature in wild Wellington. These include New Zealand Birders, Whale and Dolphin Watch – Wellington, Wild Plants of Wellington and New Zealand Native Orchids. There are also two excellent online citizen science projects that can help you find species of interest, called *eBird NZ* (for bird sightings) and *iNaturalist NZ* (for all species). These are also free to join and easy to use, and allow you to contribute your sightings to their databases, which researchers can then use to study species distributions, abundance and trends. To help with bird identifications, the *eBird NZ* website offers a free-to-download app called Merlin with an NZ Bird Pack available.

The photographs in this guide also help with making accurate identifications. Because many of the same species appear in different chapters, there is usually only one image of a species in the book, searchable by using the index.

THE NATURE RESTORATION CAPITAL

The publication of this guide describing the wildlife and wild places of the wider Te Upoko-o-te-Ika metropolitan area is timely as we witness a resurgence of nature. These places are havens for countless natural wonders, which together make this part of Te Ika-a-Māui North Island unique and special.

The protections for wildlife and plant life afforded by the various nature reserves and marine reserves described here are an important part of actively restoring the ecology of the natural world, and a tangible expression of a sense of kaitiakitanga. They embody collective actions to protect and care for the taonga and mauri contained within them through te kawa innovative actions that draw on western science and mātauranga Māori.

This guide will hopefully help to amplify this kaupapa and encourage the growth of a sense of kaitiaki, by helping readers to discover, appreciate and respect the natural taonga of wild Wellington.

The nature of wild Wellington has undoubtedly changed since it was given its English name in 1840. Sadly, some notable species that were present then are now

Tī kōuka cabbage tree and view of the south coast.

extinct, including the huia, North Island piopio, whēkau laughing owl, mātuhituhi bush wren and koreke New Zealand quail.

Other species were lost as breeders here, such as kākāpō, kōkako, tīeke saddleback, weka and hihi stitchbird, while some only persisted at the periphery or on Kapiti Island, such as kākā, red-crowned kākāriki, kārearea New Zealand falcon, tītitipounamu rifleman and toutouwai North Island robin. All of these except the kākāpō have now either been reintroduced here or have returned to the capital naturally as breeding species.

Thanks to the collective conservation mahi of recent decades, kākā and kārearea New Zealand falcon can now be seen flying over the CBD, kiwi pukupuku little spotted kiwi and takahē can be heard calling once again not far from the Beehive, hihi stitchbirds are breeding at Zealandia and Kapiti Island, tīeke saddleback, tītitipounamu rifleman and toutouwai North Island robin are breeding outside Zealandia's fence, and kōkako and weka have been successfully introduced and are breeding at Kapiti Island. And there are plans to bring the kākāpō back at the proposed Puketahā ecosanctuary near Wainuiomata.

Some large remnants of native forest are regenerating and other native habitats are recovering through the efforts of ecological restoration projects, many of which bring together mana whenua, community groups, local and regional government and the Department of Conservation (DOC).

The restoration project at Zealandia is well known, but it is by no means the only one. Me Heke Ki Pōneke Wellington City Council and the Ōtari–Wilton's Bush Trust are working to restore the best example of the original lowland podocarp forest in the capital; the Remutaka Conservation Trust has brought back kiwi-nui North Island brown kiwi in the wild near Wainuiomata; the multi-stakeholder Capital Kiwi Project has started returning kiwi-nui to a 20,000-hectare pest-controlled area to the west of the capital; and Forest & Bird's Places for Penguins project is providing nest boxes for kororā little blue penguins on the coast.

Predator Free Wellington, its various affiliated suburban groups around the city, and other volunteer groups (among them MIRO in Muritai Eastbourne, the Matiu Somes Island Charitable Trust, the Waikanae Estuary Care Group, the Friends of Mana Island, and the Friends of Otari–Wilton's Bush Trust) have also been working in parallel to help control and ultimately eradicate invasive predators across the whole area.

The ambitious plan for a predator-free Wellington is already well advanced in that rats, mustelids and possums have been eradicated from Miramar Peninsula, Rongotai, Lyall Bay and Kilbirnie. Predator-free groups are now extending the pest trapping network into Island Bay, Hataitai, Berhampore, Ōwhiro Bay, Newtown, Melrose, Southgate and Matairangi Mt Victoria. Next it will be extended into the rest of the city.

Mana whenua (Taranaki Whānui, Te Āti Awa and Ngāti Toa Rangatira), the Greater Wellington Regional Council, Wellington City Council, Porirua City Council, Hutt City Council, Upper Hutt City Council, Kapiti District Council and many community groups are also undertaking animal pest and weed control operations and planting native species in the wider area from

Tūī on flowering wharariki flax.

Waikanae in the north to Te Rae-akiaki Pencarrow Head in the south. Vital conservation work by DOC, mana whenua and volunteer community groups is also restoring native species at the three largest offshore islands in the area: Matiu, Mana and Kapiti.

Important scientific research is being done by Te Papa curators and scientists, sometimes in conjunction with others, including scientists at DOC, Crown research institutes, Te Herenga Waka Victoria University of Wellington, Ōtari-Wilton's Bush Reserve and alpine plant collection curators at Percy Scenic Reserve.

The Taputeranga Marine Reserve on the south coast, established in 2008 as the first no-take marine reserve in a capital city anywhere in the world, and the even larger marine reserve between Kapiti Island and Waikanae sandspit (established in 1992), are also helping to restore marine wildlife and ecosystems. It is hoped that all of these unfolding conservation success stories will continue to inspire others.

Taken together, the dozens of wild places featured in this book also demonstrate how wild Wellington is more than the sum of its parts. This complex miracle of nature, which scientists call an ecosystem, is an evolving, self-replicating network of living organisms. In te ao Māori, it is a taonga treasure unified by the mauri life force of all its connected parts.

WILDLIFE WATCHING RULES AND ETIQUETTE

When it comes to watching wildlife and enjoying wild nature, most people exercise common-sense 'etiquette'. Wildlife watching activities and nature reserves are governed by various laws, but these are not always widely known. It is vital that we all observe the statutory rules and behave responsibly around wildlife, so it is worth recapping those that are most relevant in the context of this guide.

First and foremost, do not harm any native species protected under the Wildlife Act, and do not deliberately introduce any invasive plant or animal into the wild.

The rules that cover watching marine mammals include keeping at least 20 metres away from seals on land. Getting too close may panic them, and if they stampede they can injure themselves, or may become aggressive, especially if you block their 'escape route' back into the sea. On land they can move as fast as people and they have a powerful bite that can cause serious infection. They need time to rest on land, so please do not deliberately disturb their sleep or try to touch or feed them. Always observe any rules for dogs. If dogs are permitted in a reserve or on a beach, keep them on a leash well away from any seals.

On the water, if you are in a boat and you see dolphins or whales, it's important to stay back and give them space to avoid stressing or displacing them. This includes not disturbing or harassing them, or making loud noises near them, or feeding them. It is a legal requirement to stay at least 50 metres away from any cetacean, and at least 200 metres away from any baleen or sperm whale mother and calf. Please do not swim with whales, or with dolphins that have juveniles with them. Boats are allowed to gradually increase their speed to outdistance dolphins but must not go faster than 10 knots until more than 300 metres away from them. If you are planning to swim at a beach or river, you can check on the water quality at www.lawa.org.nz/explore-data/swimming.

Please also observe the rules at the Taputeranga and Kapiti no-take marine reserves, where fishing (including spear-fishing) and shellfish gathering are prohibited. It is also illegal to take or hold the empty shells of many native snail species without a permit.

Birds have not evolved to digest the same foods as humans, so the wrong foods can make birds sick or kill them. For example, if kākā are fed nuts or seeds they can develop metabolic bone disease. Ducks can also develop wing deformities from eating bread.

So, please don't feed wildlife, even if a bird or an animal comes to you and seeks to eat your food.

Please heed any roped-off or signposted area as it may be a nest site for a threatened bird species, such as dotterels or falcons. Be aware that kārearea New Zealand falcons may dive at people near their nest site and can cause injury with their sharp talons. Not all bird nesting sites are roped off, so please be alert when walking on sand dunes or beaches and avoid deliberately disturbing birds there, including gulls. For example, birds get stressed when they are chased by dogs, so please control your dog/s to prevent that happening. If dogs are not permitted at a site, as is the case at Waikanae sandspit, please do not take them with you.

It is illegal for a member of the public to remove any native plant growing on Crown land or in a public reserve, or on any public road, without official permission, or without the consent of the owner or occupier of the land if it is on private land. Please also take care not to trample native habitats in protected areas, and always tread with care to minimise any disturbance of native habitats.

Native orchids have high conservation value, so their flowers should not be picked. The New Zealand Native Orchid Group has published a code of conduct for native orchids on its website, which covers matters such as the taking of seeds from common species for cultivation.

A NOTE ON PLACE AND SPECIES NAMES

This book covers Wellington City, the harbour, and the wider metropolitan Wellington area as far north as Kapiti Island and east to Kaitoke Regional Park in the Tararua Ranges foothills. There are three te reo Māori names used throughout the book for the city and the region: Pōneke, which refers to both Wellington city and Wellington Harbour and is thought to be either derived from a mis-transliteration of 'Port Nick' (Port Nicholson) or shortened from pō nekeneke, meaning 'journey into the night', regarding the exodus of Te Āti Awa from Pipitea; Te Whanganui-a-Tara, 'the great harbour of Tara', which refers to Wellington Harbour; and Te Upoko-o-Te-Ika-a-Māui (the head of the fish of Māui), the southernmost part of of Te Ika-a-Māui North Island including Wellington, referring to the fishing up of the island by Māui.

Most place names are given in te reo Māori as well as English, although not all locations have a translation: for example: Te Awa Kairangi Hutt River; Plimmerton beach; Mākara. Similarly with species names, te reo Māori and English common names are used throughout. Māori sometimes used the same word for two or more different species (e.g., kuaka, mākaka), some terms (e.g., toroa) are both 'umbrella' and specific, and there are often no Māori words for recently introduced or vagrant species. The index includes all Māori and English species names mentioned in the text.

PŌNEKE
WELLINGTON CITY

He oranga wai, he oranga tangata: As waterways thrive, so too do people	21
1. Zealandia Te Māra a Tāne	24
2. Ōtari–Wilton's Bush Reserve	34
3. Wellington Botanic Garden Ki Paekākā	44
4. Te Ahumairangi	52
5. Mount Tarikākā and Khandallah Park loop track	58
6. Pōneke Wellington waterfront	64
7. Matairangi Mount Victoria	72
8. Waimapihi Reserve	78

Ko Pukeariki tōku mounga
Ko Korokoro-o-Te-Mana tōku awa
Ko Pukeariki tōku marae
Ko Te Tatau o Te Pō tōku pouwhare
Ko Ngāti Tāwhirikura, ko Ngāti Te Whiti ōku hapū
Ko Te Āti Awa tōku iwi
Ko Liz Mellish ahau

It is my pleasure to provide some kōrero celebrating the wild Wellington experience. We will journey through Pōneke Wellington City, to the south coast and then north to Te Awa Kairangi Hutt Valley. Rather than take you through an extensive history I have chosen to give some short insights into the way mana whenua inhabit this landscape. It is my hope that this will become a tohu guide for the future.

Our journey began with the ōhākī a Te Wharepōuri, the dying words of Te Wharepōuri, to illustrate the responsibility handed down to us from our rangatira. He spoke to Hōniana Te Puni-kōkopu from his deathbed, giving him the mantle of leadership for our people in Te Whanganui-a-Tara. We continue to live by that creed today.

HE ORANGA WAI, HE ORANGA TANGATA:
AS WATERWAYS THRIVE, SO TOO DO PEOPLE

Liz Mellish MNZM, Amokura, Te Wharewaka o Pōneke

Zealandia Te Māra a Tāne, a former water-catchment site, is one of the best places to meet our flora and fauna in a truly accessible way. Te Āti Awa whānau have been involved in this project since its inception, joining in the fundraising for the predator-free fence and supporting the kaupapa with appointments at governance and operational levels. We have assisted in the transfer of animals including tuatara and kiwi. Through the Ahu Whenua trusts we still have representation, and it has been exciting to see passionate whānau working there as a career.

Ōtari-Wilton's Bush is next door to Zealandia, and they complement each other so well. These gardens are a museum for the endemic flora of Aotearoa, where young and old can celebrate the diversity of our flora and fauna. There are some majestic trees, including Moko, the female rimu who is a mokopuna of Tāne Mahuta, our god of the forest. The Māhanga Stream flows from Zealandia and passes through Ōtari on its way to join Korimako Stream to become Kaiwharawhara Stream, an interweaving waterway that provides a safe place for tuna eels to be present and visible at Ōtari.

Adjacent to Ōtari is a block of land still covered with original forest that is in Māori land title but landlocked and inaccessible. A fortunate partnership, albeit an accident rather than a plan.

Wellington Botanic Garden Ki Paekākā symbolises the joy of the partnership between mana whenua and Wellington City Council. The name acknowledges the prevalence of kākā in the city and provides a kōrero for a beautiful garden. It hosts collections of exotic species and flower gardens alongside native species, creating a space that allows whānau to enjoy the beauty and peace of a unique botanic display. Pipitea Stream originates here and flows through the gardens, visible in small glimpses.

To round off this area of Te Whanganui-a-Tara we travel to Te Ahumairangi, the impressive mounga that embraces the central business district of Wellington. The mounga is part of an area known now as the town belt which, while disputed by mana whenua, nevertheless has provided a wonderful habitat for people, flora and fauna. The city is fortunate to have this protected forest land, although an ongoing blight for mana whenua is that these streams are mostly hidden from view, having been culverted and diverted as drains in the early days of European settlement; however, their stories are gradually being told. Named streams include Te Aro/Waimapihi, Waikoukou, Kumutoto, Tutaenui, Waipiro, Pipitea, Tiakiwai, Whakahikuwai, Pakuao, Te Waipaekākā. Premier House, the official residence of the prime minister, has a spring that has been used to provide water to the Old Government Buildings on Bunny Street and Lambton Quay, but also importantly was used by our tohunga over the years when undertaking rituals requiring a cleansing ceremony.

On the lower slopes, Northland and Orangi Kaupapa were the sites of large cultivation areas that supplied Kaiwharawhara Pā, Pipitea Pā and Ōhariu. These areas were selected to take advantage of good sun and soil and access to water.

Whairepo Lagoon on the waterfront is named after the eagle rays (also known as whai keo) that take refuge there from the visiting maki orca and aihe dolphins. The kororā, little blue penguins, are another unexpected source of joy for waterfront visitors as they return home to their nests in the lagoon. The building on the lagoon is Te Raukura, Te Wharewaka o Pōneke, and is near the original site of Te Aro Pā. It houses a conference centre, café and waka house. Waka crews take pride in caring for the lagoon and share with visitors their knowledge about the animals that live there.

The graving dock in front of Te Papa allows young tuna eels to enter the Waitangi Stream and travel in the underground stream up to the Basin Reserve. In Waitangi Park, named for the stream, the rushes give the baby eels a home and sanctuary as they travel. Waitangi was an extensive wetland before development of the city and the area has been redeveloped to emulate that environment.

Matairangi Mount Victoria is also known as Tangi te Keo, referring to the pūrākau story of Ngake and Whātaitai, the two taniwha who live in the harbour. When Ngake broke through the cliffs that blocked the lake from the ocean beyond, creating the harbour, Whātaitai became stranded and died, having failed to breach the land himself. His soul flew as a bird to the top of Matairangi and mourned there. Matairangi has been extensively built upon and is host to three streams which flow into the Waitangi Stream. At its southern end is the Akatarewa Pā site and below that the Basin Reserve and former cultivations called Hauwai.

Completing the Pōneke Wellington City section is the Waimapihi Reserve. It is named for the wahine Mapihi who bathed in the stream of the same name, and flows from the hills of the reserve down to Te Aro. In 2012 a historic culvert for the stream was unearthed at the Z service station on Vivian St and a memorial to Mapihi was created by sculptor Ra Vincent (Te Āti Awa) using the clay from the culvert. Mapihi is also the subject of the largest sculpture in Aotearoa, a celebration of Māori women: a massive work undertaken by New Zealand artist Shona Rapira Davies.

This statue of Kupe with his wife, Hine-te-aparangi, and his tohunga priest, Pekahourangi, stands in front of Te Wharewaka.

View of the upper lake, Roto Māhanga.

1 ZEALANDIA TE MĀRA A TANE

Zealandia Te Māra a Tāne in Karori was the first fully fenced, pest-free urban ecosanctuary in the world, and now ranks as one of Aotearoa New Zealand's flagship ecological restoration projects. Since it was launched in 1995, it has become one of the most popular wild places in the country to see taonga bird species in their native habitats.

Zealandia is located in a 225-hectare valley of lush regenerating native forest within an 8-kilometre predator-proof fence. It has extensive regenerating native forest (including hīnau, māhoe and kōtukutuku tree fuchsia), a wetland area, and two large freshwater lakes – Roto Māhanga and Roto Kawau – connected by the Māhanga Stream. Eighteen rare or threatened native wildlife species have been reintroduced to Te Māra a Tāne – the garden of Tāne – which makes it an excellent place to see kiwi pukupuku little spotted kiwi, kākā, takahē, tīeke saddleback and hihi stitchbird.

The remarkable diversity of native birds here also includes the vociferous tūī, the serene kererū New Zealand pigeon, the jittery red-crowned kākāriki, the shy pāteke brown teal, the melodious korimako bellbird, the charming toutouwai North Island robin, the fearless kārearea New Zealand falcon, the gregarious pōpokotea whitehead and the inscrutable ruru morepork.

You can often see tūī feeding on nectar from wharariki coastal flax in flower along Lake Road in spring and summer. When you do, check out the green-blue iridescence on their feathers and the way the orange pollen rubs onto their head, allowing them to pollinate the flowers. Watch out, too, for korimako feeding on nectar from the yellow-green flowers of the kōtukutuku during August–December. While they feed, the bright purplish-blue pollen rubs onto their head. After pollination, the flowers turn red and stop producing nectar and then start to produce their purple-red berries or kōnini. Mature kōtukutuku grow along Te Māhanga Track (near the upper lake) and by Roto Māhanga, and there is one next to the kākā feeders on Tūī Terrace.

The mercurial hihi – 'ray of sunshine' in te reo Māori – was extinct on the mainland from the late nineteenth century until a new wild population was re-established at Zealandia in 2005. It is now found throughout the valley here. Sit or stand quietly near one of the sugar feeders to listen for its high-pitched *titch* calls and wait for one to fly in to drink. The black-headed male has a bright yellow neck, and can raise his two white ear tufts during aggressive territorial displays. Zealandia is the only place to see hihi on the mainland in this part of the motu.

The tīeke was extinct on the mainland from the early twentieth century until the first new wild population was re-established at Zealandia in 2002. This striking black songbird has a chestnut saddle across its back and bright red fleshy wattles. It bounds through the forest and along the ground in search of food alongside Lake Road and the Swamp Track, and has a woodpecker-like habit of hacking into rotten wood to get wood-boring grubs. To find it, listen for its rapid repeated *cheet te-te-te-te* call. It is the

Male hihi stitchbird singing.

Pāteke brown teal pair.

Adult tīeke saddleback.

Pōpokotea whitehead singing.

Adult toutouwai North Island robin.

closest living relative of the extinct huia. Zealandia and the adjacent Waimapihi and Wright's Hill reserves are the only wild places to see it on the mainland in this part of the motu.

One of the most engaging taonga forest birds, the enchanting black-and-white toutouwai is often seen by the forest tracks where it sometimes approaches closely. Scraping aside any leaves on the track often leads to a close encounter. If you stand still, you may see one enlarge the small patch of white feathers above its bill.

Aotearoa's smallest taonga bird is the tiny tītitipounamu rifleman. They were extinct as a breeding species in the capital from the early twentieth century until 60 were translocated from the Puketahā forest area in Wainuiomata to Zealandia in 2019. They belong to the endemic New Zealand wren family, an ancient lineage thought to have separated from other songbirds 80 million years ago, about the same time that the Zealandia continent started drifting away from the southern supercontinent of Gondwana.

These hyperactive green fluffballs constantly flit around flicking their wings while foraging up tree trunks and along branches. If you cup your ears with your hands and listen intently, you may hear their high-pitched *zip-zip-zip* calls and see one along the Beech Track or Swamp Track. Tītitipounamu began breeding here in 2019 and have started to disperse and nest at other sites outside the fence, such as Te Ahumairangi and Waimapihi, that have pest control. They have also been seen foraging in the Botanic Garden and Ōtari–Wilton's Bush Reserve.

The endemic pōpokotea is a white-headed, sparrow-sized songster with large eyes and a stubby black bill. It was extinct in Pōneke until reintroduced here from Kapiti Island in 2001–2; today, small flocks rove around the forest and bushes by the tracks, so watch out for them hanging upside down by their feet as they look for small insects. Their old English name of 'bush canary' is apt. Listen out for the male's melodious, canary-like whistles and trills, *viu viu viu* and *zir zir zir*. Zealandia is the most reliable place to see them in the capital.

Since 18 captive-bred birds were released in 2000–1, pāteke brown teal have bred here every year except 2002 and are now thought to have a self-sustaining population. Check for them on both lakes and the wetland area. The drake has an iridescent green crescent on both sides of the head, a chestnut breast, and an iridescent green panel on each wing.

Growing up to 30 centimetres and 1.3 kilograms, kiwi pukupuku is the smallest of the five kiwi species, and is found only at a small number of offshore islands and Zealandia, so this is the only wild place in the world where this flightless nocturnal forest bird can be seen on the mainland. Since 40 individuals were released here in 2000–1, the resident population has grown to about 200 and they are now heard and seen increasingly often during guided night tours.

Kākā, the large endemic forest parrot, was extinct as a breeding species in the capital from the early twentieth century. Fourteen were released here between 2002 and 2007; since then, hundreds of chicks have been banded here, and kākā are now the fifth most frequently seen native forest bird in the annual city-wide bird counts organised by Wellington City Council. This charismatic parrot grows up to 44 centimetres and weighs up to 400 grams. It is instantly recognisable from its loud, repeated *ka-aa* flight call and harsh *kraak* alarm calls and whistles, and you can often see one flying overhead or hanging around the feeding stations by Tūī Terrace and Lake Road.

Close views reveal the red-orange underwings and deep crimson belly. Like its alpine cousin, the kea, the kākā has a versatile 'Swiss Army knife' of a bill with a long sharp point. It can multitask with this to dig out wood-boring grubs, crunch up forest fruits, strip bark and score trees for sap, delicately feed its chicks and preen its feathers. Kākā can even use the bill as a third foot to help them climb around trees. They are also strong flyers; in 2022 one bird in the upper North Island was tracked making a 1000-kilometre round trip around the Hauraki Gulf and Waikato.

The South Island takahē was thought to be extinct until rediscovered in Te Rua-o-te-Moko Fiordland in 1948. A similar but taller species called the moho formerly occurred in Te Ika-a-Māui North Island but became extinct in the 1890s. Takahē were introduced to Zealandia in 2017 as an equivalent species to take the place of the missing moho. There are two pairs here, one of which is often seen feeding by the wetland area at the south end of Roto Kawau. The largest (up to 50 centimetres) and heaviest (up to 3.5 kilograms) of the living rail species, the takahē is a charismatic relict of the giant flightless birds that formerly roamed Aotearoa. The Te Upoko-o-te-Ika area is now a stronghold for them, with translocated birds on Mana Island and Kapiti Island and in Zealandia, which is the only wild place to see them on the mainland in this region.

All of these successful bird reintroductions have played a vital role in increasing the number of native and endemic bird species in Pōneke over the past two decades. Nearly half of those now found in Pōneke were first reintroduced at Zealandia.

The endemic kārearea New Zealand falcon is the apex daytime predator here. With so much pest control around the capital, it has naturally recolonised the city over the past two decades and has been breeding at Zealandia since 2005. Listen out for its loud *kek-kek-kek* calls and watch for it flying overhead, especially above Tūī Terrace and Roto Māhanga, or

Kiwi pukupuku little spotted kiwi is the smallest of the five species of kiwi.

Adult takahē stretching its wing, showing off its 'pāua shell' colours.

PŌNEKE

Young ruru morepork sunning itself.

Tuatara emerging from its burrow to bask in the morning sun.

perched in the tall pines near Roto Kawau.

The native ruru is the apex nocturnal predator. This golden-eyed hawk-owl can sometimes be seen roosting by day near the Beech Track or the Round the Lake Track. At night it feeds on flying insects such as moths, sometimes hovering to catch them under artificial lights. Listen out for its *ruru* or *more-pork* calls at night.

There are also several endemic reptiles and frogs in the ecosanctuary. The spiny-backed tuatara is the only living member of an ancient order of reptiles which once had a global distribution. While the rest became extinct around 65 million years ago, tuatara survived in isolation in Aotearoa. After the arrival of introduced predators, they became restricted to offshore islands until a new wild population was re-established on the mainland at Zealandia in 2005. Adult tuatara are greenish-brown and grey, and can grow up to 80 centimetres long and weigh up to 1.3 kilograms. There is a fenced research area next to Lake Road where tuatara and the smaller kōkōwai spotted skink and glossy brown skink bask near the fence on sunny days.

Growing up to 5 centimetres long, Te Hoiere pepeketua Maud Island frog is the largest of the country's four primitive endemic frog species. After it became restricted to Te Hoiere in the Marlborough Sounds, the first wild population was established on the mainland at Zealandia in 2006. This is the only place to see it in Te Upoko-o-te-Ika. Since it is nocturnal, the best time to see it is during a guided night tour.

Rōpū Tiaki, the guardianship and co-governance group of Taranaki Whānui ki Te Upoko o Te Ika and Greater Wellington Regional Council for the Parangarahu Lakes Area, has also contributed to protecting the mauri of two aquatic species at Zealandia with its translocations of kākahi freshwater mussels and toitoi common bully from Lake Kōhangapiripiri to Roto Māhanga in 2022 and 2023. Monitoring here for toitoi in October 2023 discovered one guarding eggs as well as a huge banded kōkopu and kōura freshwater crayfish.

The endemic Cook Strait giant wētā is most likely to be seen during a guided night tour. It was extinct on the mainland for over a century until 100 were transferred here in 2007. You can see the smaller Wellington tree wētā inside the wooden wētā 'hotels' by Lake Road and Tūī Terrace, and cave wētā are also sometimes seen on the guided night tours.

There are plenty of iconic native plants, too, including golden-flowering kōwhai along Lake Road and the Swamp Track, purple-white flowering mākaka native broom near the research area and Tūī Terrace, and whauwhaupaku five-finger by Lake Road, which flowers pinkish-white in June–August and then produces bunches of small, fleshy, dark purple fruits in August–February.

There is a tall tawhai red beech tree where the Beech Track branches off Lake Road. The bench near the feeder here is a good spot to watch for hihi, korimako, tīeke and toutouwai. One of the smallest native plants, the maroon and white flowering spurred helmet orchid grows among the roots of the tall tawhai tree in May–June, and tutukiwi greenhood orchids flower along the right-hand branch of the Beech Track in October–November.

You can also see a good variety of beautiful native ferns, including the endemic ponga silver fern and mamaku black tree fern, which, at up to 20 metres tall, is the largest of the native tree ferns. Both species grow by Te Māhanga Track, Beech Track and Swamp Track. There are also some lush ground ferns, such as mouku hen and chickens fern, titipo sweet fern and butterfly fern, in the forested areas along Te Māhanga Track and Round the Lake Track.

Butterfly fern – the name refers to its fan-like paired leaves.

GETTING THERE/AROUND

You can get a track map at the visitor centre. From the entrance the main track runs along Lake Road to the south end of Roto Kawau and is suitable for wheelchairs. A right-hand turn onto a pontoon walkway takes you past a lakeside kāruhiruhi pied shag colony to a takahē feeding station and a wetland area that connects with Te Māhanga Track. Lake Road continues through a gate past the tuatara research area and Tūī Terrace to the upper feeders. The Swamp Track rises to the right, up to the upper lake and the Round the Lake Track, and there are many other connected tracks that let you explore more of the valley.

ADDITIONAL INFO

Zealandia is managed by Karori Sanctuary Trust, a not-for-profit community-led organisation. It is the only mainland site in this book with an entry fee. Opening hours are 9am to 5pm every day except Christmas Day. It is worth a visit at any time of the year, but still days during the warmer spring and summer months are better for seeing most of the birds. There are guided day and night tours, and schools can arrange group visits.

Mākaka common native broom flowering.

The delicate pattern of the titipo sweet fern.

The Kaiwharawhara Stream valley.

2 ŌTARI–WILTON'S BUSH RESERVE

A visit to Ōtari–Wilton's Bush Reserve and Native Botanic Garden is an amazing experience, thanks to the rich diversity of native plants and birds in its old-growth lowland broadleaf podocarp forest. The abundance of life here is a reminder that in te ao Māori, Papatūānuku is the source and sustainer of the land and all that depends on it.

Ōtari–Wilton's Bush Reserve is the only place where you can see such a diversity of Aotearoa New Zealand's native plant flora, with over 1200 species growing within the 100 hectare reserve and its 5 hectares of native botanic gardens. This is about half the total number of native vascular plant species found in Aotearoa.

With its 800-year-old rimu and other big old trees, such as mataī, miro, tōtara and northern rātā, this is an ideal place to discover some of the taonga native plants of the wider Te Upoko-o-te-Ika area. Sensory experiences include the sublime fragrances of creamy white kohekohe and purple-white mākaka native broom in flower, and the feathery feel of the fronds of native ferns.

To explore here, start by picking up a free map from the main entrance at 150 Wilton Road. The reserve has five main tracks plus a couple of circular walking routes that wind through an extensive area of native forest including the Māhanga branch of Kaiwharawhara Stream. There is an alpine tarn, an alpine rock garden and a fernery near the entrance where kōtare sacred kingfishers are sometimes seen and blue damselflies dart about over the water in summer. From here the entrance track runs west to the visitor centre.

Local endemic plants include the world's smallest and largest species of fuchsia. The smallest – kōnini New Zealand creeping fuchsia – grows

Kōtukutuku tree fuchsia flowers.

Flowering kōnini creeping fuchsia.

on the ground near marker number nine just before the visitor centre. In summer, kōnini produces its small, bright orange and green flowers with vivid purplish-blue pollen. The largest – kōtukutuku tree fuchsia – grows on the other side of the short track that runs down to the right just before marker number nine. Its beautiful flowers appear between June and December, enticing tūī and korimako to feed on their nectar. There are larger specimens of kōtukutuku by the track alongside the Māhanga branch of Kaiwharawhara Stream.

From the deck by the visitor centre, you can see some of the larger forest trees, such as kahikatea, mataī and tōtara, plus examples of smaller tōwai, whau and tree ferns. A forest canopy walkway connects the deck to the Leonard Cockayne Centre and the native plant collections area (named for the botanist who started the collection in 1926). The canopy walkway runs 20 metres above the ground, taking you alongside the upper storey of some very tall tawa, rewarewa and tree ferns.

The tall trees here with olive-sized, dark purple fruits during October–March are tawa (the name has come to mean 'purple' in te reo Māori). Kererū like eating these fleshy fruits and play a crucial role in dispersing them through the forest. Watch out, too, for the attractive red flowers of rewarewa and the white-flowering rātā vine in summer, when you may spot korimako bellbirds and both kahukōwhai yellow admiral and kahukura red admiral butterflies, which sometimes feed on the vine's nectar. The tall female kahikatea near the walkway produces colourful small orange and purple fleshy, fruit-like seed cones in winter.

Past the Leonard Cockayne Centre is an area of cultivated native plants in a rock garden. Kererū often feed on kōwhai here in spring and summer. The summery white flowers of rauhuia native flax linen and rock harebell brighten up this area, and tawny mokomoko northern grass skinks sometimes bask here on sunny spring mornings.

The nearby lookout has a panoramic view across the valley where you can watch for kākā and kārearea New Zealand falcon flying over. Listen out for their loud calls and watch for them in the trees around the edge of the garden area below the lookout. From here you can continue down through the native gardens where tūī, kererū and sometimes pīpīwharauroa shining cuckoos feed on or among the

Kahikatea growing near the boardwalk.

Rewarewa flowering.

Tawa fruit.

Kahikatea produce these small, colourful, range and purple fleshy fruit-like seed cones in winter.

Moko, the giant 800-year-old rimu.

abundant kōwhai in spring and summer.

Left of the track by the very tall kauri, there is a specimen of one of the rarest taonga tree species in Aotearoa, rātā moehau Bartlett's rātā. Only 13 adult trees are known in the wild, so this cultivated one is a valuable seed source. In December–January its ethereal, pale pinkish-white flowers attract a constant flow of bees.

The track runs downhill to the Troup Picnic Lawn, where there is a small wooden bridge over the stream. This is a good spot to see tuna eels and check overhead for passing native birds such as kārearea and kererū, or to see the northern rātā that tower over the north-facing slope above the valley with their spectacular crimson flowering in December–January.

Surveys show a healthy diversity of native freshwater fishes in the stream, including giant, banded and short-jawed kōkopu, kōaro, īnanga, blue-gilled bully, and both tuna short-finned and ōrea long-finned eels. You may also see some of the bigger tuna swimming around when the water is clear.

From the picnic area follow the signs up through the native forest to the 800-year-old giant rimu, a taonga tree named Moko.

To coincide with Matariki in 2021, Pōneke's oldest and tallest tree was gifted the te reo Māori name Moko by local iwi Te Āti Awa. The name was selected as being the most appropriate for a female tree younger than Tāne Mahuta, the largest living kauri, located in Te Tai Tokerau Northland. Liz Mellish of Te Āti Awa explains, 'Ōtari is whenua that is important to Te Āti Awa and Ngāti Tama as a site of indigenous forest which was a place for bird snaring. It was on the route to Mākara and trails went past and through there. All trees of Tāne are important in te ao Māori; the ngahere forest was the home of insects, birds and plants that provided sustenance for us. Not only sustenance but rongoā [medicine] and building materials, clothing and many other uses such as weapons, carving, and waka. The value we place on the ngahere is immeasurable for mental health as it's a place for reflection, for gathering with whānau, and to commune with living flora and fauna.'

The forest tracks take you through kohekohe forest and stands of big rimu and miro, some of which have impressive perching lilies or peka-a-waka bamboo orchids, or vines such as akakaiore New Zealand passionfruit or kareao supplejack, growing on them.

There is a platform with benches in front of Moko where you can view this majestic tree festooned with perching ferns, lilies and orchids and now the rare kohurangi Kirk's tree daisy, which was once extinct in the capital but recently returned to Ōtari. Small songbirds like riroriro grey warbler and pīwakawaka New Zealand fantail seem as tiny as

Kererū New Zealand pigeon.

Kākā.

Flowers of rātā moehau Bartlett's rātā.

Mouku hen and chickens fern.

Kaihua New Zealand jasmine flowering.

insects as they flit around the foliage of this forest giant. Moa once stepped over Moko's roots, and forest birds such as the huia, mātuhituhi bush wren and whēkau laughing owl once lived among her branches. Although those species are now extinct, kererū, red-crowned kākāriki, tūī and korimako can all be seen in the reserve today, and kākā sometimes forage on the ground near Moko, searching out fallen forest fruits and seed cones.

The kererū is another forest giant, growing up to 50 centimetres and weighing up to 630 grams, which makes it one of the largest and heaviest forest pigeon species in the world. Watch for kererū feeding on forest fruits and flowers, or, during the breeding season, males flying up over the forest before making a steep skydive. Listen out, too, for the chattering calls of dainty red-crowned kākāriki. Their emerald-green feathers are good forest camouflage, but you may see one perched on a branch at the edge of the forest, or in flight.

Continuing uphill past Moko, you pass more giant rimu growing among the kohekohe, tree ferns and ground ferns. Aotearoa has an impressive diversity of native ferns. There are about 200 species, some 60 percent of which are found in Te Whanganui-a-Tara. Ōtari has a good variety in the forested areas. There are tree ferns, such as ponga silver fern and mamaku black tree fern; some impressive ground ferns, such as mouku hen and chickens fern and heruheru crepe fern; and several filmy fern species, with irirangi drooping filmy fern being common on the forest floor in places. More is still being learned about the ferns of Aotearoa. For example, Te Papa botany curator Leon Perrie has described new species in recent years.

When kohekohe flowering peaks in May–June, the forest is alive with tūī and korimako feeding on its nectar, and the air is filled with the spicy sweet fragrance of its creamy white flowers. You can either follow the track uphill here until it loops back down to the picnic area, or turn around and retrace your steps back down there.

The remnants of kohekohe, tawa and hīnau here are the best examples of original lowland podocarp forest in the capital, and a valuable seed source for regenerating areas and the eventual restoration of the forest across the city. Other plants you might see or smell include kaihua New Zealand jasmine, porokaiwhiri pigeonwood, kiekie and tātarāmoa bush lawyer.

Look around for the fallen red fleshy, fruit-like seed cones of rimu and miro from October–March, and tawa fruit during December–March. Tawa fruit is so large, the kererū is the only bird in the reserve able to swallow it and, likewise, the similarly large orange fruit of the karaka.

Both kākā and kākāriki are doing well in the lowland podocarp forest here at

Ōtari, feeding on abundant forest fruits and breeding in its many natural nesting sites. Kākā select holes in large trees such as hīnau, while kākāriki can use holes in smaller trees such as kōtukutuku and tī kōuka cabbage tree. In recent years a kākā pair have nested in a hole inside one of the big old trees. In summer 2022/23, during the egg incubation period I watched from a safe distance and saw an adult kākā fly down onto the trunk and peer inside the nest hole. Shortly after, a second adult kākā emerged and climbed up the trunk, and then the first bird entered the nest hole and the second bird flew off. Watch out, too, for kākāriki coming and going from their smaller nest holes in spring and summer. They seem to like tī kōuka here.

The average number of native bird species counted in the capital has increased by about 40 percent since 2011; along with Zealandia, Ōtari is one of the main wild places supporting their increase. For example, since 2011 numbers of kererū counted across the capital have tripled and the kākā count has increased by 260 percent. The growing abundance of bird life here has undoubtedly been helped by the proximity to Zealandia, and by Ōtari having its own pest control network for the past 30 years.

Research on native orchids is also being carried out here by conservation and science adviser Dr Karin van der Walt and Te Papa botany curator Dr Carlos Lehnebach, who are studying ways of germinating and storing native orchid seeds to help with their conservation. The other plants being studied are the critically endangered rātā moehau, kauri, and the rare endemic parasitic flowering pua o Te Rēinga wood rose. There are also specimens of the rare stalked adder's tongue fern and some of the common greenhood orchid species growing in the reserve's plant nursery.

I have also seen ngahere geckos in the vicinity of the native plant collection area. With their other-worldly 'goggle' eyes and vertical pupils, these small, intricately patterned reptiles are from an ancient lineage that first evolved some 200 million years ago. Here in Aotearoa, geckos and skinks are adapted to relatively cold temperatures, so they produce fewer young and breed less often, and are slow-growing – rather like kākāpō. They are also unusual, in global terms, in that they give birth to live young rather than lay eggs.

There is plenty of wonderfully weird insect life here in summer, including kapokapowai New Zealand bush giant dragonflies by the stream, kahukura and kahukōwhai butterflies in the open areas, and pēpeke nguturoa giraffe weevils and flightless stick insects in the forest canopy and understorey. Some of the interesting fungi growing beside the tracks up to Moko in autumn and winter include orange waxgill, harore lemon honeycap *Armillaria limonea* and various colourful coral fungi.

Ngahere gecko basking.

GETTING THERE/AROUND

The main entrance is located at 150 Wilton Road, about 5 kilometres from the city centre. The number 14 bus from the city centre stops near the entrance here, and there are parking areas at the Wilton Road and Churchill Drive entrances. The main path from Wilton Road to the visitor centre is suitable for wheelchairs, as is the canopy walkway to the Leonard Cockayne Centre. There are bike racks at the main entrance.

ADDITIONAL INFO

The Ōtari-Wilton's Bush Trust organises periodic guided walks to see birds, plants, insects and fungi, puts on public talks, and arranges different options for volunteering, all of which are notified online and via social media. There is also an annual open day in September when the reserve sells interesting native plants from its nursery.

Kohekohe in flower in Wellington Botanic Garden Ki Paekākā.

3 WELLINGTON BOTANIC GARDEN KI PAEKĀKĀ

The oldest legally protected area in the capital is also one of the best if you enjoy watching tūī flying over while you sip your coffee in the café by Lady Norwood Rose Garden. For a closer encounter with a tūī, take a walk from the café up through the kohekohe forest along the Serpentine Walk.

The irrepressible tūī is the larger of Aotearoa New Zealand's two remaining taonga honeyeater species, reaching up to 30 centimetres long and weighing up to 125 grams. It is unique in having two curved white feather poi or tufts on its throat. It can use its syrinx or 'voice box' to sing hundreds of fluid, complex songs, and is able to fine-tune the airflow from each of two bronchial tubes so that either side is closed or open. This allows a tūī to duet with itself. Its vocal range is so great it includes ultrasonic tones, beyond human hearing.

One of the best times to do the walk is when the kohekohe forest flowers heavily in May–June. This memorable forest spectacle offers a chance to see an abundance of native birds. The flowers fill the forest with their subtly sweet, spicy fragrance, and their nectar attracts tūī, korimako bellbirds and kākā to feed on them – and in return the birds pollinate the kohekohe.

A member of the mahogany family, kohekohe has tropical characteristics such as large leaves and cauliflory, or the production of fruit and flowers directly from the trunk and woody branches. The creamy white flowers produce grape-sized green fruits containing orange-coloured seeds, which birds such as kererū, tūī and korimako feed on once the fruit ripens and opens. The radiant kōwhai near the rose garden feed the same bird species in September–October.

Tūī feeding in kohekohe.

Kohekohe fruit.

Big, old black maire (centre) with ponga silver ferns.

The three kohekohe forest remnants in the Botanic Garden also have tītoki, hīnau, karaka and rewarewa, and there is a big old black maire tree signposted along the Pukatea Bush Walk which produces its yellow-orange fruits from December to April.

The 25-hectare Botanic Garden was established in 1868 and is now managed by Wellington City Council, which has been controlling animal pests here for years. It is also an excellent place to see the curving koru and graceful fronds of the common native fern species, especially along the Pukatea Bush Walk, Waipiro Bush Walk, Mamaku Way and Mānuka Path, and in the Fernery. The garden is home to about 40 native fern species, ranging from tree fern giants to the petite fork ferns and delicate filmy ferns.

The eye-catching filmy ferns have a lush green palette of translucent fronds. Common in wet forest habitats, they form the largest fern family in Aotearoa. One of the commonest is irirangi, the drooping filmy fern, which grows along the Mamaku Way section of Pukatea Bush Walk. The largest filmy fern, matua mauku, grows near Serpentine Way and Mamaku Way. The latter also has ponga silver fern, mokimoki fragrant fern, rereti lance fern and the rare maidenhair fern.

Irirangi drooping filmy fern.

Rereti lance fern.

Fork fern on a tree fern.

Matua mauku filmy fern.

The small drooping fork fern *Tmesipteris elongata* is one of the few surviving members of the primitive order Psilotales, which thrived 400 million years ago. A few can be seen along the Mamaku Way, growing on the trunk of a tall tree fern next to the stream.

Native orchid species here include winter greenhood orchid, which grows on the ground in the kohekohe forest between Camellia Valley and the top of the Waipiro Bush Walk in May–June. Some impressively large peka-a-waka bamboo orchids grow on native trees in the garden, including one near the Founders' Entrance and one near Mamaku Way. In October–November, they produce sprays of small creamy yellow flowers with a spicy sweet fragrance.

A large summer-flowering winikā orchid grows on a big branch over the track through the Fernery, and both the maikuku common sun orchid and tutukiwi greenhood orchid flower here in November–December. The former grows on a grassy bank by the wide sealed track between the rock garden and the Treehouse, while the latter grows by the narrow unsealed track that passes under tall exotic pines and connects the Duck Pond with the Magpie Lawn. This track also has spleenwort ferns and clubmoss.

In addition to abundant tūī and kererū, you should also expect to see kākā and red-crowned kākāriki in the garden. Kōtare sacred kingfishers are sometimes seen near the stream, and pūtangitangi paradise shelduck sometimes roost at the Duck Pond. In June 2023, I found two unbanded male tītitipounamu rifleman foraging in the area below the Treehouse, which were likely to be the offspring of the birds now breeding at Zealandia. I have also seen kārearea New Zealand falcons swoop down to catch small songbirds near the rose garden and the Treehouse, and perch on top of the exotic pines near the Treehouse.

Native birds are present year-round, with a notable period of activity in winter when akakaiore, the native passionfruit vine, produces its grape-sized orange fruits near the Serpentine Track, in Camellia Valley, and in the forest above the Fernery. Tūī, kākā, korimako and

Collared earthstars.

Tutukiwi greenhood orchid flowering.

Peka-a-waka bamboo orchid on tree trunk.

Akakaiore native passionfruit in fruit.

Peka-a-waka bamboo orchid flowers have a delicious spicy sweet fragrance.

The titiwai glowworm is an endemic fungus gnat that produces a blue-green bioluminescence.

Male tītitipounamu rifleman singing near the Treehouse.

tauhou silvereye feast on them.

The interesting insect life here includes luminous titiwai glowworms, pinky-sized Wellington tree wētā, fluttering kahuku monarch butterflies, flightless stick insects, and singing kihikihi wawā cicadas. To see the titiwai glowworms, join one of the monthly summer evening tours that are notified on the noticeboard by the Founders' Entrance and via social media.

There is also the chance of seeing some interesting fungi by the tracks in autumn and winter, such as collared earthstars, ruby bonnets, the local endemic chanterelle mushroom *Cantharellus wellingtonensis* and the poisonous red-capped fly agaric toadstool, an introduced species.

Armillaria mushrooms.

GETTING THERE/AROUND

There is easy public access via the number 2 bus that runs along Lambton Quay to the Founders' Entrance and the West Entrance along Glenmore Street, or the cable car from Lambton Quay, or on foot from The Terrace through Bolton Street Cemetery up to the rose garden. There is limited parking near the rose garden. Free maps are available at the main entrances and the Treehouse Visitor Centre. The top of the cable car, Lady Norwood Rose Garden and the Glenmore Street main entrance are wheelchair friendly. Visitors are spoiled for choice here with so many tracks and paths. There is a child-friendly playground area and a café by the rose garden. The garden is open to the public every day, dawn to dusk.

View of the capital from Te Ahumairangi.

4 TE AHUMAIRANGI

Te Ahumairangi rises 300 metres above sea level, dwarfing the high-rise buildings and CBD. The main features of this 100-hectare area of the town belt are the Paehuia ridgeline and the south-east facing escarpment. The lookouts at both ends of the maunga offer impressive vistas of the city, harbour, and surrounding landscape.

One of the te reo Māori meanings of Ahumairangi is 'whirlwind'. The ridgeline of Te Ahumairangi was known to Māori as Paehuia, according to the nineteenth-century ethnologist Elsdon Best, possibly in reference to the now-extinct endemic huia that once lived in its original crimson-flowering cloak of northern rātā forest.

About half of Te Ahumairangi is now covered in a regenerating patchwork of mostly māhoe forest with kohekohe, rewarewa, mamaku tree ferns and smaller ground ferns. Near Bank Road there is also a native forest remnant of tītoki and hīnau with ngaio, wharangi and māhoe. Secondary forest of māhoe, ngaio, whauwhaupaku five-finger and tarata grows alongside the original forest remnant, and there is northern rātā, poroporo and kawakawa. The rest is dominated by exotic pines and macrocarpa. The regenerating native forest extends down the lower slopes, studded with ponga silver fern and various smaller common ground ferns.

Wellington City Council (WCC) is gradually removing the tall exotic pines and, along with the volunteer group Te Ahumairangi Ecological Restoration (TAER), replacing them with native podocarp species, including large-scale planting of northern rātā at the north end, and rimu in some east-facing gullies. Over 10,000 native trees have been planted.

Te Ahumairangi also has a network of

Poroporo flowers.

self-setting pest traps supplied by WCC and Greater Wellington Regional Council (GWRC). This and other pest control activities in adjacent areas are maintained by TAER, Zealandia, Predator Free Northland and RAMBO (Rats and Mustelid Blitzing Ōtari).

The Paehuia Ridgeline Track winds from the south-west to the north-east, punctuated by tall trees and panoramic views to the west and north including Mount Tarikākā, the western suburbs, Zealandia, Ōtari–Wilton's Bush and some of the Mākara wind farm turbines.

There is an extensive network of signposted walking tracks on the south-east facing slope, which is part of the city's Northern Walkway – some of these are quite steep in places. Most are unsealed and can be muddy when wet, so wear

Ponga silver fern.

Tītoki flowers.

Kawakawa fruit.

The lemon-scented flowers of tarata lemonwood.

View to the ridgeline of Te Ahumairangi.

practical footwear and take care.

In recent years kārearea New Zealand falcons and kākā have returned to nest in forest on the maunga. Other native birds often seen here are kererū, tūī, pīwakawaka New Zealand fantails and tauhou silvereyes, and kōtare sacred kingfishers and red-crowned kākāriki are also sometimes seen. Ruru call at night and pīpīwharauroa shining cuckoos are often heard calling in spring or early summer.

A pair of tītitipounamu rifleman that bred successfully on the maunga in the summer of 2021/22 are thought to have been the first to breed here in more than 100 years. They reportedly raised two broods, fledging nine chicks that summer. The male was recognised from its colour leg bands as having hatched at Zealandia 3 kilometres away, where 60 tītitipounamu were translocated in 2019.

The best time to look for these tiny forest birds is during the warmer part of the day. Listen for their high-pitched *tseep tseep* calls and watch for them rapidly climbing tree trunks and branches feeding on small insects and spiders, sometimes close to the ground. If you see one, watch for its hyperactive wing-flicking. The male is a brighter green than the female, which is a more muted fawn-green with speckling on the breast.

The best time of day to watch and listen out for kārearea is between about 10am and 2pm when they are most active. Kākā are often most active early and late in the day, making their loud screeching calls as they fly between Te Ahumairangi and the Botanic Garden.

There are some very interesting native orchids here. The green bird orchid has been found growing near the start of the northern end of the Ridgeline Track and near the lookout at the southern end, flowering in October–December. A number of native spider orchid species grow at the northern end, including *Corybas vitreus*, described by Te Papa botany curator Carlos Lehnebach in 2016, which flowers in August–September. Maikaika common onion orchid, raupeka Easter orchid, *C. trilobus*, maikuku common sun orchid and tutukiwi greenhood orchid also grow here, mostly at the northern end, flowering in spring or summer.

A modest variety of the smaller native ground ferns can be found by the tracks, such as pānoko thread fern, kiokio palm-leaf fern, kōwaowao hound's tongue fern and petako sickle spleenwort.

The maunga also has its own tiny, critically endangered endemic freshwater snail species, *Potamopyrgus oppidanus*, measuring just 3 millimetres long. The rare native moth species *Chersadaula ochrogastra*, last collected from Breaker Bay in 1923, was found on Te Ahumairangi in 2021, so this appears to be its last known habitat.

Some of the other moths you may see here include the lime-green pūriri moth and the delicately patterned green māhoe moth. Kahuku monarch and kahukōwhai yellow admiral are the most commonly seen butterflies, and pepe para riki, Māui's copper and North Island glade copper have also been recorded here. Among the larger insect species here are rō New Zealand giant stick insect, kapokapowai New Zealand bush giant dragonfly and Wellington tree wētā.

An interesting selection of autumn mushrooms grow here including ruby bonnet, austral honey mushroom, jewelled amanita and the introduced poisonous red-capped fly agaric toadstool.

Pānoko thread fern.

GETTING THERE

The number 13 and 22 buses stop along Northland Road about 300 metres from the southern start of the Ridgeline Track. There is limited parking at the southern end (by Stellin Memorial Park) and northern end of the Ridgeline Track, and along Weld Street.

Pīpīwharauroa shining cuckoo.

Pepe para riki North Island glade copper butterfly.

Green bird orchid in flower.

Petako sickle spleenwort.

Kōwaowao hound's tongue fern.

View from the maunga summit looking across the city to the south coast.

5 MOUNT TARIKĀKĀ AND KHANDALLAH PARK LOOP TRACK

Rising 445 metres above sea level, Mount Tarikākā above Khandallah Park is one of the two highest points in the capital. It has panoramic views across the harbour and the Remutaka Range – and on clear days you can sometimes see the snowcapped peak of Tapuae-o-Uenuku in the Kaikōura Ranges in Te Waipounamu South Island. The sky towers above you here – in te ao Māori, the realm of Ranginui.

Tarikākā is the original te reo Māori name for what was mistakenly called Mount Kaukau by Pākehā, kaukau being a mispronunciation of kākā. Tarikākā is said to mean 'where the parrots rested'.

Kākā were reportedly abundant on the maunga before the native forest was burned off in the nineteenth century, after which they became scarce. A new wild population was introduced at Zealandia between 2002 and 2007, and pest control activities began targeting brush-tailed possums in this area, organised by local volunteer group Predator Free Khandallah. As a result, kākā are now seen and heard more often in the remnant native forest on the east slopes of Mount Tarikākā.

Higher up, where the landscape is more exposed with rocky outcrops and grassy tussocks, be on the lookout for the two raptor species, kārearea New Zealand falcon and kāhu swamp harrier. The kārearea is the smaller of the two and is most often seen in the fast flux of flight. In contrast, the kāhu has a more languid, gliding flight. The kārearea has faster wingbeats, up to about 120 per minute, compared with the kāhu with up to about 60 per minute.

One way to explore here is to walk the 4-kilometre clockwise circuit of the Skyline Walkway Track that starts at the end of Woodmancote Road just past the Khandallah public pools. The track rises through remnant native forest in

Makomako wineberry flowering.

Tātarāmoa bush lawyer vine fruiting.

Tātarāmoa bush lawyer vine flowering.

Khandallah Park over a small bridge that crosses Tyers Stream. After a distance of about 800 metres the terrain becomes open and more exposed. After another 300 metres it reaches the TV mast and maunga summit lookout.

Once you've taken in the panoramic vista, follow the track east along the ridgeline of the Skyline Walkway for about 500 metres and then turn right at the fork and follow the Skyline Walkway Track downhill, back to the public pools at the top of Woodmancote Road.

The track rises up about 250 metres in elevation from the public pools to the maunga summit and includes some steep sections, so it takes 2–3 hours to walk, depending on the pace you set. The best time is during the warmer months on a relatively still, clear day, as strong wind gusts can make the exposed sections more challenging.

The remnant native forest here has mature māhoe, tawa, kohekohe and kōtukutuku tree fuchsia, with a dense understorey including makomako wineberry, tī kōuka cabbage tree and rangiora tree daisy.

The forest has a rich variety of native ferns, including the veined bristle fern, which grows on the trunks of tree ferns such as ponga silver fern and whekī rough tree fern. Ground ferns here are especially diverse, with such forest jewels as mātātā lace fern, titipo sweet fern, butterfly fern and raurenga kidney fern.

Female kahuku monarch butterfly.

Kahukōwhai yellow admiral butterfly basking in the sun.

Watch out for kapokapowai New Zealand bush giant dragonflies near Tyers Stream.

Among the native orchids, peka-a-waka bamboo orchid grows on trees in the forest and tutukiwi greenhood orchid by the track. On the higher terrain, keep an eye out in summer for green bird orchid, leek orchid and New Zealand mountain greenhood. Maikuku common sun orchid, maikaika common onion orchid and small onion orchid have also been found growing in the vicinity of the maunga summit and TV mast.

Scarlet rātā vine and tātarāmoa bush lawyer weave their way through the low, bushy tauhinu cottonwood and coprosma shrubs, but take care not to brush the ongaonga stinging nettles by the track, with their distinctive serrated light green leaves and small, pale stinging hairs. Ongaonga is the preferred food plant of the kahukura red admiral butterfly, which can sometimes be seen gliding around or basking with its wings open on warm, still summer days.

Kōura freshwater crayfish, which can grow up to 7 centimetres, live in Tyers Stream, and a few native freshwater fish species have been recorded in the area, including banded kōkopu and kōaro.

Listen out for the whoosh of kererū and tūī in flight, the squeaky calls of the pīwakawaka New Zealand fantail and tauhou silvereye, and the pretty trills of the riroriro grey warbler. You might also hear the chattering of red-crowned kākāriki, the pealing chimes of a korimako bellbird or the whistle of a pīpīwharauroa shining cuckoo. Ruru morepork call in the forest after dark.

There is a kaleidoscope of native butterflies here in summer, including three small pepe para riki copper species – Māui's copper, North Island glade copper and North Island coastal copper. Check also for the larger kahukōwhai yellow admiral and kahuku monarch. The Australian vagrant painted lady butterfly is also sometimes seen here. Other interesting insect life for the sharp-eyed observer to watch for in the forest here includes kapokapowai New Zealand bush giant dragonfly, Wellington tree wētā, ground wētā and prickly stick insect. Ngāokeoke, the New Zealand peripatus or velvet worm, has also been recorded here: an unusual small creature that looks like a velvety caterpillar with two antennae and a platoon of stumpy legs.

Autumn rains can bring out some wonderfully weird fungi in the forest here, such as white basket fungus, collared earthstars, austral honey mushroom and various colourful waxgills.

GETTING THERE

For public transport, the nearest railway stations are Khandallah and Box Hill, both about a 600-metre walk from Khandallah public pools on Woodmancote Road. There is limited parking by the pools.

View north from Te Papa along the waterfront towards Te Ahumairangi.

6 PŌNEKE WELLINGTON WATERFRONT

The scenic city waterfront walk from the harbour ferry ramp by Queens Wharf to Oriental Bay is an invigorating way to see the scale of the capital's dramatic harbour setting, and a chance to see some of the local wildlife, especially the seabirds, marine mammals and stingrays that sometimes visit the waters of the inner harbour.

Porpoising pods of aihe common dolphins sometimes come into the inner harbour in summer, often followed by a flock of tara white-fronted terns as they chase schools of aua yellow-eye mullet and mohimohi pilchard, which is a spectacular sight. The agile aihe drive the small fish closer to the surface, which brings them into plunging range for the flock of tara.

Check the water for kororā little blue penguins, too. They have nested under the wharves in this area and are sometimes seen swimming near Te Papa and Chaffers Marina, in Whairepo Lagoon and off Oriental Bay beach.

Swift flocks of pakahā fluttering shearwaters sometimes also fly and swim through this area in pursuit of schools of small fish. They catch fish by pursuit diving, using their partially folded wings to swim underwater, and can catch krill by 'snorkelling' forward at the surface with their wings raised and head submerged as they search underwater. They are sometimes joined in these feeding frenzies by the large, yellowish-headed, white-bodied tākapu Australasian gannet, which can dive from a great height like an arrow into the water to catch fish.

Watch out, too, for any long-whiskered, snub-nosed kekeno New Zealand fur seals as they can sometimes haul out on the rocks between Frank Kitts Park and Whairepo Lagoon, or swim around offshore in winter and spring. A rare subantarctic fur seal was regularly seen basking by Customhouse Quay in August–September 2016, and there is a record of a rare Antarctic Weddell seal at Whairepo Lagoon on 29 June and 3 July 1937.

Pods of black-and-white maki orca are sometimes reported in this part of the harbour. In December 2022 and January 2023, maki sightings were reported weekly as pods worked their way around the harbour, passing near Te Papa. Earlier sightings near Te Papa were reported between the months of August and December in 2022, 2020, 2012 and 2011.

Kororā little blue penguin.

It's always exciting to see these fearless mega-dolphins, also known as killer whales, in the harbour. The bull maki, with its tall, straight dorsal fin, typically grows to 6–8 metres long and weighs 5–6 tonnes, while the slightly smaller cow has a smaller, recurved fin. Like humans, maki can live for 60–80 years and have complex social bonds and hunting behaviours.

Paikea humpback whales and tohorā southern right whales also make occasional appearances. Two big paikea swam past Te Papa along to Oriental Bay on 11 June 2023. An adult was seen swimming a few metres off the wharf next to Te Papa on 1 May 2020, and a young paikea was seen near Aotea Quay from the inter-island ferry on 28 April 2020. Paikea, recognisable by their long, narrow pectoral fins, can grow up to 17 metres and weigh up to 40 tonnes.

Tohorā were so common in the harbour in the 1840s that, when they bred in the calmer bays, some early Pākehā colonists complained of being kept awake at night by their loud, growling calls. More recently, a big bull tohorā famously wowed Wellingtonians during 3–10 July 2018, swimming around and breaching along the waterfront to Oriental Bay and Evans Bay. It featured in news reports that referred to it by the name Matariki. Another tohorā swam around here and into Evans Bay during 25–26 July 2023,

Subantarctic fur seal.

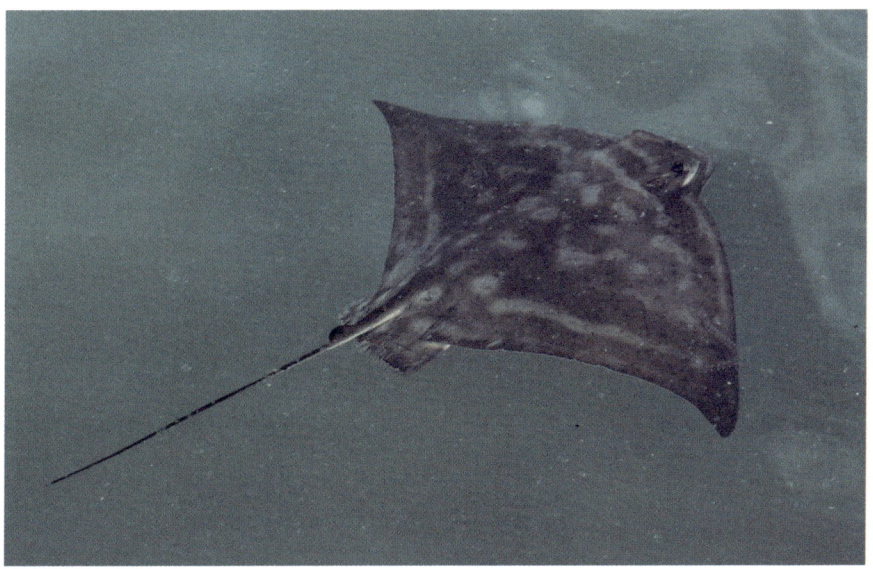

Whai keo eagle ray in the shallows.

Tohorā southern right whale tail flukes.

Maki orca passing off Oriental Bay beach.

Tohorā southern right whale head.

Paikea humpback duo off the waterfront.

captivating hundreds of whale-watchers with its deep, growling calls and views of its huge head and tail flukes. It was seen again in Island Bay a day later before it swam off towards Pariwhero Red Rocks. Adult tohorā can grow up to 15–18 metres long and typically weigh around 50 tonnes. They can be identified by the large white callosities on their head, which are inhabited by whale lice.

The waterfront walk takes in the area from the harbour ferry terminal past Queens Wharf and Frank Kitts Park to Whairepo Lagoon, alongside Te Papa, then the Waitangi Park wetlands and Chaffers Marina to the seawall by the Port Nicholson Yacht Club marina, and on to Freyberg Beach and Oriental Bay beach.

Rāpoka leopard seals have been reported as annual visitors in the capital in recent years. A large one hauled out for the day by Port Nicholson Yacht Club marina on 23 July 2019. Hundreds of seal-watchers came to see it after photos were posted to the Whale and Dolphin Watch – Wellington Facebook group. Another, which hauled out and stayed at Oriental Bay beach during 26–28 September 2023, was reportedly given the te reo Māori name Kōanga (Spring) by the naming komiti of Taranaki Whānui ki Te Upoko o Te Ika.

A young bull ihupuku southern elephant seal, dubbed Blossom by reporters, came ashore to moult at Oriental Bay beach in November 1962, returning in November 1963 for six weeks according to Dr Robert Falla, the director of the Dominion Museum (now Te Papa) at the time. An estimated 20,000 Wellingtonians flocked to see Blossom one weekend. Elephant seals are the largest of all the seal species. Adult bulls can grow up to 6 metres long and weigh up to 4 tonnes.

More recently, a 2-metre taha pounamu blue shark delighted onlookers when it was seen swimming around below the high diving platform on Taranaki Wharf, near Te Papa, on 10 April 2015. Whairepo Lagoon can also be a good place to see whai keo eagle rays and koinga rig houndsharks swimming in the shallows in summer.

The *Bush City* exhibition outdoors at Te Papa is a great short walk for children to explore. It re-creates some of the country's native habitats with plantings of rimu, rewarewa, kōtukutuku tree fuchsia, puawānanga native clematis, tī kōuka cabbage tree and various ferns, and includes a re-creation of a cave system with a 'glowworm' display. The elevated lookout area has panoramic views of the harbour, and a few common native forest birds also visit it, such as tūī, pīwakawaka New Zealand fantail and tauhou silvereye.

Te Papa's *Te Taiao Nature* exhibition celebrates the unique natural environment of Aotearoa and showcases many of the native species that call Te Upoko-o-te-Ika their home. After visiting Te Papa,

The kororā little blue penguin is the world's smallest penguin species.

Rāpoka leopard seals can use their teeth to sieve krill.

Ihupuku southern elephant seal, the world's largest seal species.

Koinga rig houndshark in the shallows.

Adult tara white-fronted tern in non-breeding plumage.

Puawānanga native clematis.

Bush City at Te Papa.

continue along the waterfront towards Chaffers Marina and you will find what renowned ecologist Geoff Park called the 'remnant ecologies' of Waitangi Park behind Te Papa, which attempt to replicate some of the native habitats of the capital's original coastline.

Next to that is Clyde Quay and Port Nicholson Yacht Club marina where whai keo eagle rays, whai short-tail stingrays and koinga rig houndsharks can be seen when they come in to swim and feed in the shallows in January–February. Tara white-fronted terns sometimes roost on the adjacent marina sea wall.

It is a short walk from here to Freyberg Beach and Oriental Bay beach below the northern slope of Matairangi Mount Victoria. Whai and koinga also come in to the shallows here on summer evenings, usually in January–February. A pod of five maki was also seen passing the beach on 27 October 2022, and before that a pod of seven on 2 January 2019.

GETTING THERE

Many of the bus routes in the capital pass along Lambton Quay and Courtenay Place near the waterfront. The number 14 connects Oriental Bay with the city centre, and Wellington railway station is about a 200-metre walk from Queens Wharf. The waterfront area is suitable for wheelchairs.

View from Matairangi across to the city centre.

7 MATAIRANGI MOUNT VICTORIA

The spectacular 360-degree view from the maunga is compelling enough to visit Matairangi Mount Victoria at any time of the year. The large lookout platform located 196 metres above sea level here has a bird's-eye view north-west over the harbour to the central city and Te Ahumairangi. You can also watch out for kārearea New Zealand falcons in the warmer months.

Y ou can walk up to the summit from the north or the south, or you can catch a number 20 bus to the top from either end and then walk back down. From Oriental Bay a track zigzags steeply up to the lookout area. The main footpath up from the Newtown end is longer but more gradual and has many side tracks.

Over half of this 45-hectare area of the town belt is dominated by exotic conifers, shrubs and grass, planted since the late nineteenth century. The rest is mostly native forest and shrubland with about 10 percent comprising native plantings, which are helping to bring back tūī, kākā, kererū New Zealand pigeon and kārearea to the maunga.

The kārearea is a special taonga bird on the maunga. The town belt's avian apex predator can reach up to 200 kilometres per hour when it folds its wings and dives to catch prey. Its return to the city is another conservation success story. Kārearea self-reintroduced to the capital in 2005 with the first recorded nesting at Zealandia, and since then they have spread out across the city and the southern suburbs.

Several pairs now breed within the town belt area, with foraging territories that include the central city, bringing their distinct *kek-kek-kek* calls back to the skies above the capital. Reports with photos of these brilliant aerial predators standing in city gardens and parks plucking and

Adult male kārearea New Zealand falcon with prey.

eating their prey are now regularly posted on social media.

In the summer of 2020/21 a pair nested on the ground near a track within a few hundred metres of the summit, in a spot where the council put up signage to warn walkers there was a pair nearby, and that kārearea can sometimes dive-bomb passers-by. This was good advice because kārearea can inflict serious wounds with their razor-sharp talons, especially if they rake your head. If one dives at you, duck and cover your eyes, and make a hasty retreat.

On a visit here in February 2021, I stayed on the track so as not to disturb the birds, and was rewarded with memorable views of both adults standing on branches above the nest and their still slightly fluffy juvenile making its first attempts at flying.

Another highlight was hearing the adult male calling as he flew in to land on a nearby branch, seemingly to signal to the juvenile he was bringing food, and then watching the juvenile emerge from the pile of logs around the nest. The male then flew down onto one of the logs with a dead songbird in his bill. With wings raised he presented the bird to the juvenile, which bowed and held its wings down, fanning out its tail. The handover lasted a few seconds before the male flew off. The juvenile took the prey and glided down onto the ground nearby where it devoured its meal in a few minutes, repeatedly gulping down small gobs of flesh. After that, it sat down in a shady spot for a snooze.

A pair was regularly seen on the Carillon Tower by Pukeahu National War Memorial Park in winter 2023, sometimes flying from the tower over towards Matairangi. Watch out, too, for adult ruru moreporks, which can have up to three fluffy juveniles in the forest with them here during December–January, or listen for them calling at night in the Majoribanks Street area near Kent Terrace.

The Mt Victoria Bush Regeneration Group has been removing invasive plants and, along with Mt Vic Revegers and the Rotary Club of Wellington, has contributed to native forest regeneration with a focus on planting māhoe, akeake, māpou and taupata mirror bush. Also active are the local Predator Free Mt Vic backyard trapping group and Mt Victoria Vermin Trappers.

Karaka and mānuka are among the more familiar native trees here. The purple flowers and orange fruits of poroporo add a splash of colour, and koromiko hebe, tī kōuka cabbage tree and rangiora tree daisy add some 'flower power'. The common māhoe whiteywood grows on the slopes where its small purple berries attract tūī and kererū, and this is also a stronghold for the uncommon thick-leaved māhoe. Native ground ferns growing in the understorey include kōwaowao hound's tongue fern,

Kahukura red admiral on koromiko hebe flower.

Native bees feeding on mānuka flowers.

Female kārearea New Zealand falcons grow up to a third larger than the male.

Juvenile kererū New Zealand pigeon.

Australian sandy stiltball mushroom.

blue shield fern and pukupuku rasp fern.

As the native bush returns, kākā are increasingly heard and seen flying overhead, and be sure to listen out for pīpīwharauroa shining cuckoos calling during their spring migration from Melanesia to Aotearoa in October–December. Tūī, kōtare sacred kingfishers, warou welcome swallows and the smaller bush birds – pīwakawaka New Zealand fantail and riororiro grey warbler – are also seen here. Kererū, in particular, enjoy feeding in the tall eucalypts.

Watch too for small flocks of tauhou silvereye foraging in foliage for small insects and listen for their melodic warbling and trilling. These tiny green-olive songbirds have a silvery-white eye ring, grey back, and creamy-grey underparts with buff-pink on their flanks.

Flowering koromiko hebe attract an abundance of 'miniature marvels', including native bees and hoverflies, and kahukura red admiral and kahukōwhai yellow admiral butterflies in the warmer months near the southern end of the Matairangi nature trail. The microcosmos of insect life here also includes kapokapowai New Zealand bush giant dragonfly, smooth stick insect and kihikihi wawā chorus cicada. Species that are easier to see in the forest at night by torchlight include the giant stick insect, Wellington tree wētā and huhu longhorn beetle.

The tauhou silvereye is easily recognised by its green-olive colour and silvery-white eye ring.

An interesting first New Zealand record of the sandy stiltball, an exotic fungus, was found recently growing under a macrocarpa here by Te Papa scientist Lara Shepherd. Careful observation by the tracks could also be rewarded with sightings of collared earthstars, the white basket fungus, the exotic poisonous red-capped fly agaric mushroom and the native puapua-a-Autahi anemone stinkhorn fungus.

GETTING THERE/AROUND

Visitors can walk up to the summit from the north or the south, or catch a number 20 bus to the top from either end and then walk back down. There are multiple separate tracks designated for walking or for mountain biking. The Wellington City Council website has a walkway map showing the different tracks.

View from Waimapihi Reserve east across the harbour.

8 WAIMAPIHI RESERVE

This is where you can see the 'halo effect' in action as native bird species spread out naturally from inside the predator-proof fence around the Zealandia ecosanctuary. They are spilling over into adjacent Waimapihi Reserve (formerly known as Polhill Reserve), which means it is possible to see a range of taonga birds here and in the adjacent smaller George Denton Park.

Ongoing pest control is organised at Waimapihi Reserve by Ngā Kaimanaaki o Te Waimapihi, so the reserve also provides foraging and nesting habitat for some of these birds. For example, tīeke saddleback originally from Zealandia have been breeding successfully in Waimapihi since 2014, less than a kilometre from the fenceline. Tītitipounamu rifleman from Zealandia have also been seen outside the fence here, including a pair that raised two clutches of chicks in a tree hole near the Clinical Track in spring and summer 2023. Toutouwai North Island robins also bred here in spring 2023, with three pairs successfully raising their chicks.

Kārearea New Zealand falcons are sometimes seen flying over the reserve, as well as pīpīwharauroa shining cuckoos, while ruru morepork and kiwi pukupuku little spotted kiwi can sometimes be heard or seen at night from the fenceline track when kiwi walk or ruru perch nearby. Other bird species to watch out for here include kākā, pōpokatea whitehead, kererū, red-crowned kākāriki and hihi stitchbird.

The tracks in this reserve are quite steep in places, so one option is to start at the Brooklyn wind turbine and walk downhill northwards along the fenceline, watching for birds on both sides where the track runs towards George Denton Park, and then turn around and walk back up to the wind turbine.

An immature tīeke saddleback, which has not yet grown its two red wattles.

Rō brown stick insect on muehlenbeckia – all 23 stick insect species in Aotearoa are flightless.

Rō smooth stick insect on a flowering koromiko hebe.

Wellington tree wētā.

Black tunnelweb spider.

Alternatively, you can detour on the way back to the old disused Brooklyn army bunkers for panoramic views across the harbour east towards the Tararua and Remutaka ranges. At night you can also walk the fenceline watching out for geckos, Cook Strait giant wētā, stick insects and spiders on the fence using a torch. Spiders' eyes tend to show up as bluish and sparkly in torchlight.

Another option instead of walking along the fenceline to George Denton Park is to walk 800 metres down the wind turbine track to a right turn that runs about 300 metres down to Ashton Fitchett Drive. Just below where it meets the road, turn left onto the Transient Track, which descends (quite sharply in places) through Waimapihi Reserve about 3 kilometres to Aro Street. This passes through regenerating vegetation and has glimpses out across the valley, but note that the steep track here can be very muddy and slippery after rain.

Waimapihi has some notable areas of māhoe forest and kanono/māhoe scrub. A wide variety of regenerating native plants are found here including ngaio, rangiora tree daisy, hangehange New Zealand privet, kawakawa and poroporo. The ferns include mamaku black tree fern and ponga silver fern, and there is a good diversity of ground ferns including veined bristle-fern, petako sickle spleenwort and pākau gully fern. Look out too for hūperei black orchid, tutukiwi greenhood orchid and maikaika common onion orchid near the fenceline track from the wind turbine down to George Denton Park in November–January.

Since 2016, volunteers from the Polhill Protectors Ngā Kaimanaaki o Te Waimapihi, in conjunction with Wellington City Council and the Brooklyn Trail Builders, have reportedly planted more than 30,000 native plants and trees in the Waimapihi area.

Ruby bonnet.

Common basket fungus.

The fly agaric is a poisonous introduced toadstool species.

You might see skink movements by the tracks on sunny days during September–March, such as mokomoko northern grass skink, glossy brown skink and copper skink. Although very cryptic, ngahere geckos have also been reported in the area.

Cook Strait giant wētā have started spilling through the fence around Zealandia and have been recorded within Waimapihi at night, on or near the fence. Some of the other notable insect life you might see includes Wellington tree wētā and cave wētā, which can sometimes be seen on the ground, on trees, or on the fence. Stick insects including the New Zealand giant stick insect, unarmed stick insect and smooth stick insect

Despite its armour, the Cook Strait giant wētā is vulnerable to predation by rats.

may also be seen on the fence at night. During the day, kahukura red admirals, kahukōwhai yellow admirals and pepe para riki North Island glade copper butterflies can be seen on the wing in summer.

Among the fungi that sometimes grow by the tracks here are the introduced poisonous red-capped fly agaric mushroom that comes out in March–May, ruby bonnet in December–June, and white basket fungus in May–July.

GETTING THERE

The number 25 bus goes to Aro Valley, which is near the northern end of the track. The number 7 and 17 buses go along Karepa Street in Brooklyn. The nearest stops are the two closest to Ashton Fitchett Drive, which you walk up to get to the wind turbine car park and access the southern end of Waimapihi Reserve. There is car parking at the wind turbine.

HAPPY VALLEY

ISLAND

13
Te Kopahou
Visitor Centre

ŌWHIRO BAY

Tapu Te R
islan

14

PŌNEKE
KI TE TONGA

THE SOUTH COAST

TE MOANA-O-RAUKAWA
COOK STRAIT

15

Ngā tai karekare o te tonga: The turbulent seas of the southern coast	86
9. Oruaiti Reserve and Breaker Bay	90
10. Rangitatau Palmer Head and Tarakena Bay	94
11. Taputeranga Marine Reserve and coast	98
12. Te Kopahou Reserve including Spooky Gully	108
13. Te Haape Stream valley	116
14. Pariwhero Red Rocks Scientific Reserve and Te Rimurapa Sinclair Head	122
15. Te Moana-o-Raukawa Cook Strait ferry	128
16. Nicholson Canyon and Cook Canyon pelagic seabirds	132

NGĀ TAI KAREKARE O TE TONGA:
THE TURBULENT SEAS OF THE SOUTHERN COAST

Liz Mellish MNZM, Amokura, Te Wharewaka o Pōneke

Standing on the mounga of the south coast you can feel the essential energy of Te Moana-o-Raukawa Cook Strait and the Tasman Sea meeting in a collision between Te Ika-a-Māui and Te Waipounamu, the North and South Islands. This energy is a constant wero challenge to all who live and work here. It drives us to be resilient and positive and live active lives; so it is for the flora and fauna that also live here.

The Oruaiti Pā site on Motu Kairangi Miramar Peninsula rests on a large dune system, forming cliffs that protect Te Turanga-o-Kupe Seatoun from the ocean. The cliffs are covered with hardy plants, and the pā's strategic importance is apparent when you climb to the stylised waka site atop the dunes. From there you can survey the opening of the harbour to Te Moana-nui-a-Kiwa Pacific Ocean, where seabirds flock, tohorā whales pass and aihe dolphins swim alongside the vessels that ply the ocean between the main islands. Clearly this site has a pre-colonial and colonial military purpose due to its closeness to the eastern side of the harbour. Earlier hapū who lived on the fringes of the harbour at Rangitatau and Tarakena Bay used signalling by fire to advise of any incursions into the 'Heads'. Nowadays the arrival of visitors is marked by the inter-island ferries and constant movement of planes at Wellington airport.

The passage of tohorā whales must have been magnificent to witness. From here, away from the glare of the city, the night sky and whetū stars are easily viewed. Whetū were used by mana whenua for navigation, te maramataka the Māori lunar calendars, and acknowledging Papatūānuku and Ranginui as our first people. This acknowledgement is also apparent in the names of mounga and awa throughout Te Whanganui-a-Tara.

The pūrākau story of Ngake and Whātaitai, the famous taniwha who opened the passage known as the Heads and Te Au-a-Tāne to create the harbour, is important to not only Te Whanganui-a-Tara but the South Coast too. Ngake broke through the enclosure rocks to open the Heads, and Whātaitai expired after a failed attempt to breach the land at Evans Bay. His body created the flat, low-lying area called Te Awa-a-Taia, now known as Kilbirnie.

Taputeranga Marine Reserve and coast is of special cultural importance to Te Āti Awa as we had a papakāinga ancestral settlement there on the shore to protect our environment and access to the Tapu Te Ranga island from which the area gets its name. As a reserve today it is a great resource for educating our young people about diving and identifying kaimoana seafood, but not taking from here, ensuring a safe place for kaimoana to successfully grow and multiply for the future food store.

A stylised waka marks the site of Oruaiti Pā on Motu Kairangi Miramar Peninsula.

Adjacent to Taputeranga is Te Kopahou Reserve, which includes Te Haape Stream valley and the area commonly known as Spooky Gully. This reserve allows people to enjoy the ferocity of the weather and sea and the rich resource Raukawa Moana provides, making the hills and gullies great places for a wide variety of flora and fauna to thrive.

The Red Rocks area, or, as we know it, Pariwhero, and Te Rimurapa Sinclair Head have cultural significance in the pūrākau of Kupe the great Polynesian explorer who travelled to Aotearoa with his wife Hine-te-aparangi and navigator Pekahourangi on their waka *Matahourua*. The pūrākau talks of the rocks being stained red either because Kupe spilled his blood on the jagged mussels on the rocks or because his nieces, thinking his long trip to Tōtaranui in the Marlborough Sounds chasing a giant wheke octopus had caused him harm or death, are said to have cut themselves in grief. Luckily for us all, Kupe

View of Te Tauihu-o-Te-Waka-a-Māui (the top of the South Island) from Pariwhero Red Rocks.

vanquished the wheke and returned to continue exploring and naming many sites on his journey around Aotearoa.

Something you can't fail to notice when exploring the south coast is the relationship between the land and the sky, the volatile moana and the winds of Tāwhirimatea. Despite Te Waipounamu South Island being visible from the southern coastline, where close connections with whānau are maintained, these elements remind us of how difficult travel between the two main islands can be.

At the same time, Te Moana-o-Raukawa has provided an abundance of resources to mana whenua on both sides, with marine currents bringing kaimoana, both shellfish and pelagic fish, rich in all the best nutrients. The sheer diversity of marine life has enabled us to honour the cultural values of manaakitanga and offer a warm welcome and delicious kai to manuhiri guests. Here, rimurimu seaweed is respected as a home for fish to breed and thrive in, and is used by mana whenua as rongoā medicinal plants or to enrich our soil.

Deep within Raukawa Moana lies an ecosystem of canyons that have a dramatic effect on both Te Whanganui-a-Tara Wellington and Te Tauihu-o-Te-Waka-a-Māui (the top of the South Island). These canyons provide important breeding sites for hoki and other pelagic fish, and a passageway for tohorā whales to traverse along the eastern coastline of Aotearoa. As mana whenua we maintain our kaitiakitanga on protecting these canyons. Māori and mana whenua have fought against the discharge of untreated sewage from Wellington City and the Hutt Valley, and for the development at Moa Point of a sewage treatment plant. Our whānau in Te Tauihu are deeply affected by the impact of the sewage on those trenches and the hoki breeding grounds. The kaumātua often raise the matter with us, concerned that their livelihoods could be affected if we are not vigilant.

View from the reserve down to The Pinnacles.

9 ORUAITI RESERVE AND BREAKER BAY

Another iconic Pōneke site with stunning sea views is Oruaiti Reserve. Formerly known as Point Dorset, the south side of the headland looks down onto The Pinnacles at the north-east end of Breaker Bay. It also has a spectacular view of the harbour entrance channel south-east to Te Rae-akiaki Pencarrow Head and east to Ōrongorongo in the southern Remutaka Range.

The headland has shrubland and duneland habitats with adjacent shingle beaches, and on the landward side there are steep 50-metre cliffs, so take care not to get too close to the edge. There is extensive rimurapa kelp forest off the eastern side of the headland, and headland tracks can be accessed from Breaker Bay beach, the Pass of Branda or Churchill Park.

The *Dominion Post* newspaper reported that a 2.8-metre immature male mangō taniwha great white shark was found dead in a fishing net set to target blue moki near Te Tangihanga-a-Kupe Barrett Reef about a kilometre off Breaker Bay in October 2010. A protected native species, the great white was added to Te Papa's collection, where it was assessed by fish curator Andrew Stewart as being the largest mangō taniwha specimen preserved intact in Aotearoa. An examination revealed the shark had a kekeno New Zealand fur seal claw in its stomach.

These apex predator mega-sharks specialise in ambushing prey, so are very stealthy. Keep an eye out for the pods of aihe common dolphins or maki orca that sometimes pass offshore here in summer, or even a shark fin at the surface. Whales are also possible; a tohorā southern right whale was seen swimming off the coast here on 28 May 2007. The headland is also a good vantage point to watch for tara white-fronted terns, taranui Caspian terns

The mangō taniwha great white shark is a marine apex predator.

Kōtuku ngutupapa royal spoonbill.

Kawau tikitiki spotted shag.

Rimurapa bull kelp floats due to the honeycomb structure inside its leathery blades.

and tākapu Australasian gannets passing offshore, as well as Te Upoko-o-te-Ika's kawau shag species, all five of which occur in this area.

Small numbers of kawau tikitiki spotted shags, tara and tarāpunga red-billed gulls nest on The Pinnacles in spring and summer. With binoculars it is possible to see the flamboyant breeding plumage of the kawau tikitiki, including its double crest and the broad white stripes that extend down both sides of its neck. Its pale blue-grey plumage is set off by bright green-blue facial skin, blue eye rings, and yellow legs and webbed feet. A rare find among the tara flock here on 12 December 2014 was a white-winged black tern that stayed until 11 January 2015.

Watch out, too, for small rafts of kororā little blue penguins swimming just offshore; they are sometimes seen coming ashore late in the day during summer. Further out, toroa albatrosses can sometimes be seen following the bigger fishing boats into the harbour entrance channel. There are also occasional sightings of kōtuku ngutupapa royal spoonbills on the coast here during their post-breeding northward migration from Te Waipounamu. A flock of 30 was seen offshore flying low over the sea heading towards Pito One Petone in April 2017. In flight, kōtuku ngutupapa hold their neck outstretched and trail their legs behind, which makes them look rather awkward, like a Dr Seuss cartoon bird.

Te Motu Kairangi – Miramar Ecological Restoration and Predator Free Miramar are two groups that are restoring native habitats, and they have been successful in eradicating most invasive predators around the peninsula including rats, possums, stoats and weasels. This conservation mahi is paying off, with long-absent native birds such as kererū New Zealand pigeon and red-crowned kākāriki now returning to the peninsula, and big increases in the numbers of pīwakawaka New Zealand fantail and riroriro grey warbler. A scarce cirl bunting was photographed north of the point in September 2021.

GETTING THERE/AROUND

The number 2 bus runs near this area and there are some limited parking spaces by Breaker Bay. Several tracks on the headland can be accessed from Breaker Bay beach, the Pass of Branda or Churchill Park. Be aware that the far end of Breaker Bay beach is a popular spot for nudists.

View of escarpment habitat with wharariki coastal flax by Tarakena Bay.

10 RANGITATAU PALMER HEAD AND TARAKENA BAY

From the southern end of Breaker Bay, it is about a kilometre south along the roadside coastal path to Rangitatau Palmer Head, which is a frequent haunt of seabirds and kekeno New Zealand fur seals. This southernmost point of the Miramar Peninsula offers commanding views over the harbour entrance and out over Te Moana-o-Raukawa Cook Strait.

Two pairs of kārearea New Zealand falcons have nested on the peninsula each summer since 2020/21 and sightings of this species have increased in the vicinity, so it is worth looking up for them flying along the ridgeline or over the coast.

Kororā little blue penguins also nest in this area and are sometimes seen swimming or preening at the surface offshore in small rafts, or coming ashore to their nest sites later in the day between Breaker Bay and Tarakena Bay in summer. One kororā tracked by Te Papa seabird researchers in 2014 swam from the harbour to the other side of Palliser Bay on daily 70-kilometre round trips. Others foraged closer to their nests, and another tracked bird swam 170 kilometres over three weeks on a single foraging trip out to sea.

The beautiful blue, green and buff-orange kōtare sacred kingfisher, and the large blue-grey matuku moana reef heron with its pale yellow bill and long greenish-yellow legs, sometimes hunt for small fish from the rocks along the coast here, and pairs of tōrea pango variable oystercatchers, with their bright orange bills, frequent the local beaches. Kākā, korimako bellbirds and ruru morepork are also returning to the peninsula, and pīpīwharauroa shining cuckoos are sometimes heard passing through in spring.

Pink-flowering horokaka New Zealand ice plant grows along the coast here, and it is worth looking for sand piripiri or

Piripiri bidibid in flower.

bidibid, a ground-hugging member of the rose family that produces striking spherical red, spiky flowers on its thin, rigid stalks in summer.

At Rangitatau and adjacent Tarakena Bay you will find duneland habitat, shore rock platforms, sand dunes and planted wharariki coastal flax. Natural vegetation here includes mākaka saltmarsh ribbonwood and white-flowering shore lobelia.

The south-facing sandy beach in Tarakena Bay is sheltered from south-easterly swells by Rangitatau. The tip of the headland is a good place to watch for roosting flocks of tara white-fronted terns, sometimes a couple of thousand birds or more, on the nearby rocks just offshore. From February to May check any flocks for the tarapirohe black-fronted tern, an endangered endemic species

Kōtare sacred kingfishers dive to catch their small fish, crab and skink prey.

A matuku moana reef heron stalking its small fish and crab prey.

that is sometimes seen among the tara while making its annual migration from Te Waipounamu breeding sites to wintering sites including Lake Ōnoke by Lake Ferry in the Wairarapa. Be alert, too, for any sleeping kekeno New Zealand fur seals hauled out on the shingle beach in winter or spring as they can easily be mistaken for a rock! If you see one, keep at least 20 metres away as it can deliver a powerful bite, and the bacteria in its mouth can cause a very serious, even fatal infection.

Here, the modified sand dunes support plenty of pink and white flowering rauparaha shore bindweed, some pīngao, kōwhangatara spinifex, sand piripiri and the uncommon thick-leaved māhoe. The stony beach and low vegetation has mokomoko northern grass skinks, especially at Rangitatau, and there have been a few reports of copper skinks and moko pāpā Raukawa geckos. Walk slowly and quietly along the rocky point and you could see a sleek mokomoko basking on a stone or piece of driftwood. Take care not to let your shadow fall on it and you may see its tawny golden, chocolate-brown and copper-coloured scales as they glint in the sun. Seen well, mokomoko look like tiny wingless dragons.

On a clear day Rangitatau can offer spectacular views across to the Kaikōura Ranges in Te Waipounamu South Island, and if you walk up to the nearby Atatürk Memorial above the headland you get an even better view.

GETTING THERE/AROUND

A return walk can be made from Breaker Bay beach to the harbour entrance at Rangitatau and Tarakena Bay, following the coastal path adjacent to the road. The nearest bus is the number 2 and there is limited parking by Tarakena Bay.

Mokomoko northern grass skink.

Kekeno New Zealand fur seal pup sleeping.

View from above Te Raekaihau Point.

11 TAPUTERANGA MARINE RESERVE AND COAST

Forget the computer-generated dragons of Middle-earth and Hogwarts because Taputeranga Marine Reserve has its own fantastic beasts, from maki orca to manaia seahorses. It is globally significant as the only no-take marine reserve in a capital city, and notable in Aotearoa for its remarkable diversity of marine life.

In te ao Māori, this is the realm of Tangaroa. The wild coast here has a varied geography of sandy bays and rocky reefs, with spectacular views to the south of the snowcapped Kaikōura Ranges in Te Waipounamu, and the Remutaka Range to the east. It is also a great place for sea-gazing and cloud-watching where even showery days can bring rainbows.

Taputeranga Marine Reserve was formally proposed by the South Coast Marine Reserve Coalition and Forest & Bird in 2000 before it was established in 2008, and covers 5 kilometres of coastal waters between Te Raekaihau Point and the disused Ōwhiro Bay quarry, extending about 2 kilometres offshore to the 40-metre depth contour.

Some 600 species of seabirds, fish, shellfish, crustaceans and seaweeds were recorded in the vicinity of the marine reserve in 2007, from kororā little blue penguins to tohorā puru blue whales. The complex underwater topography and diversity of marine habitats here support a unique and varied community of plants. For example, it is now jungled with almost 400 seaweed species, including forests of amber-brown giant rimurapa kelp that are havens for the resident wheke octopus and manaia seahorses, and underwater gardens of red, gold and green.

The adjacent rocky headlands and contoured escarpments, rising to heights of 100–200 metres, once supported tawa forest with rimu, rātā and kohekohe.

Today they are cloaked in a patchwork of regenerating coastal scrub and shrubland including tauhinu cottonwood, wharariki coastal flax and fragrant-flowering tī kōuka cabbage trees. Tūī often feed on the wharariki in spring and early summer, and on warm, still days you can hear the calls of tōrea pango variable oystercatchers above the singing of the kihikihi cicadas.

The myriad of wonderful fish species recorded along the south coast includes tāmure snapper, haku yellowtail kingfish, blue moki and kahawai. The fish here have increased in both size and diversity of species since the marine reserve was established. Mararī butterfish and pākirikiri blue cod are now less wary of divers, and kōura rock lobster are seen more often. Along with wheke and

Manaia New Zealand seahorse adult male.

manaia, southern reef squid live here, and there is plenty of rocky shoreline habitat to explore at low tide looking for pāpaka nui purple shore crabs and pātangatanga reef sea stars.

Protecting local fish populations in turn benefits other marine wildlife in the area, such as kororā and tara white-fronted terns. There has also been an increase in the number of marine mammal sightings reported via *iNaturalist* and Facebook over the past few years, most notably aihe common dolphins and kekeno New Zealand fur seals, but also maki orca.

Local ecological restoration work here has involved Wellington City Council, Greater Wellington Regional Council and the Department of Conservation working with community groups such as Friends of Taputeranga Marine Reserve and Forest & Bird's Places for Penguins group, which help protect kororā on the coast with nest boxes and pest control, and plant pīngao to help stabilise sand dunes.

Ngāti Toa and Wellington City Council are also working together on an ecological restoration project to protect threatened species on Taputeranga Island.

View of Taputeranga Island and pīngao from the Island Bay sand dune.

Black-foot pāua shell.

Pāpaka nui purple rock crab, Ōwhiro Bay.

Juvenile kōura rock lobster.

Pākirikiri blue cod.

Te Raekaihau Point and Princess Bay

There are three significant natural areas on the coast adjacent to Taputeranga Marine Reserve, starting in the west with Te Raekaihau Point and Princess Bay. The large shore platform and rocky reef system next to the shingle beach at Te Raekaihau Point make this a popular area for walkers and scuba divers, and a good place to watch seabirds.

In summer and autumn there is often a flock of tara white-fronted terns on the rocks at the point, at times up to a couple of thousand birds. These graceful, medium-sized terns are pale grey above and white below. The name 'white-fronted' refers to their forehead, where a thin strip of white separates the black bill from the black cap in breeding plumage.

From February to April, tara are regularly joined by smaller numbers of the endangered tarapirohe black-fronted tern while on their annual migration north from Te Waipounamu South Island to wintering sites in Te Ika-a-Maui North Island. Tarapirohe are smaller and darker than tara, with blue-grey plumage, orange legs and a bright orange bill. Look for them at the edge of the tara flock. The name 'black-fronted' refers to their forehead, where there is no white strip separating the black cap from the orange bill in breeding plumage.

Other terns you could see here are the chunky red-billed taranui Caspian tern, the largest of the world's tern species, and the black-billed Eurasian common tern, which is slightly smaller and darker grey than the tara with dark 'ear muffs'. In summer, flocks of pakahā fluttering shearwaters often fly past the point. Watch also for the twisting of tākapu Australasian gannets as they dive into the water, and for toroa albatrosses, which sometimes follow passing fishing boats.

There are usually a few tarāpunga red-billed gulls and karoro southern black-backed gulls here; kawau shags, matuku moana reef herons and white-faced herons fly over the point now and then. Look up and check for kārearea flying over the adjacent escarpment too.

In April 2021 I had a memorable close encounter with an immature kārearea that was standing on the shingle beach by the point, eating tiny pieces of pumice to help it digest the bones of small songbirds. It carried on doing this for ten minutes as I watched from a safe distance before it jumped up and flew inland.

Watch also for pods of svelte, coppery aihe common dolphins near the point as they chase fish into the bay and leap acrobatically out of the water and slap their tails to corral the fish. I have occasionally seen superpods of hundreds of aihe porpoising offshore here in summer.

From time to time, a lone kekeno New Zealand fur seal will come ashore to snooze by the point, and pods of maki orca occasionally come into the bay hunting for rays. A pod seen here on 19 February 2021 drew hundreds of whale-watchers.

Adult tarapirohe black-fronted tern in breeding plumage.

Tarāpunga red-billed gull.

A tohorā southern right whale was seen just west of the point on 2 September 2014, and the tohorā known as Matariki was seen just east of the point on 27 July 2018.

The fish diversity in this part of the reserve includes jack mackerel, sea perch, banded wrasse and haku yellowtail kingfish, and there are wheke and silver pāua among the rocks. A rare Pacific olive ridley turtle was found alive on adjacent Lyall Bay beach on 11 July 2016.

Vegetation at the point includes taupata mirror bush, pōhuehue New Zealand bindweed, māakoako sea primrose and wharariki coastal flax. Tōrea pango variable oystercatchers often roost here, and both tūī and tauhou silvereyes feed on the flowering wharariki up the escarpment in spring and summer.

A walk along Princess Bay brings you to a scenic sandy beach with pīngao sand dunes that overlooks Houghton Bay. This is an ideal spot for a picnic while watching a summer sunset.

Aihe common dolphin with calf.

Tōrea pango variable oystercatcher.

Houghton Bay and Island Bay

Shallow, sandy Houghton Bay is frequently visited by pods of aihe in summer, chasing fish or resting in the shallows. The local fish life includes tarakihi, araara trevally, pūwaiwhakarua scarlet wrasse and pātiki sand flounder, and there are manaia, kōura and black-foot pāua on the rocky reef.

A few rāpoka leopard seals have been recorded hauling out at or near Taputeranga Marine Reserve. One hauled out on Houghton Bay beach on 19 August 2010, and since then others have been seen on nearby Lyall Bay beach on 2 September 2013 and 10 August 2021.

There was a rare sighting of an Antarctic crabeater seal at Lyall Bay beach on 18 December 1963, and a young bull ihupuku southern elephant seal was photographed in Houghton Bay in November 1962. An unusually pale grey tohorā southern right whale was seen off the rocks here over a few days in the

Pūwaiwhakarua scarlet wrasse.

White-faced heron in breeding plumage, Houghton Bay.

Wheke New Zealand octopus, Marine Education Centre.

Kekeno New Zealand fur seal, Island Bay.

summer of 2005/6, drawing big crowds.

Continuing along the coastal path to Island Bay, there are a few hidden kororā little blue penguin nest boxes. The smallest of the world's 19 penguin species, kororā are nocturnal on land, returning ashore to their nest around dusk where they make a range of growls, screams and trumpeting calls.

Kekeno New Zealand fur seals sometimes haul out on rocks between Houghton Bay and the Island Bay snorkel trail, and a pair of tōrea pango variable oystercatchers nested in this area during the summers of 2022/23 and 2023/24, often feeding along the beach near Island Bay Surf Club.

The snorkel trail by the small car park opposite 194 The Esplanade is a handy place to discover the reserve's inshore marine life. Look out here for blennies, triplefins, kōura, wheke and southern reef squid. The excellent Island Bay Marine Education Centre, run by Dr Victor Anderlini, is 100 metres west of here at the old bait house.

Island Bay's long, sandy beach is renowned for its scenic views of Taputeranga Island. Local fish life includes pūwaiwhakarua, red scorpionfish, striped trumpeter and velvet leatherjacket. Snorkellers can also look out for manaia. Tuning in your eyes to look for their eyes is a good way to find them. These charismatic fish are easier to spot when the males turn bright yellow for a few weeks during their summer courtship period. The bay is also a good place to look for wheke and the endemic to Pōneke yellow-and-brown nudibranch or sea slug slithering around in its seaweed habitat.

Taputeranga Island is a stronghold for kororā and matuku moana reef herons, which nest on the island in summer, and its plant life includes the endemic Cook Strait māhoe. A colony of about 100 adult tarāpunga red-billed gulls nested on a large rock stack off the island in the summers of 2022/23 and 2023/24. This familiar white gull species, with its red bill and legs and silver-grey wings, is abundant along the adjacent coast.

The Island Bay sand dunes are part of an extensive dune revegetation project where pīngao, kōwhangatara spinifex, wharariki coastal flax and wī silver tussock have been planted. There would have been stout-legged moa walking in the sand dunes plus whakahao sea lions, kekeno and penguins along the beach before humans arrived. There was even a 2.5-metre giant monk seal species about 3 million years ago.

There are still kekeno on this coast, but a rare find was an Antarctic crabeater seal by the sand dune on 25 March 2015. Aihe are also frequent visitors in summer, and pods of maki sometimes pass through hunting for rays. Pods of them were seen doing just that on 29 September and 29 May 2023, 19 February 2021 and 10 June 2016. A big pod of 13 that swam around the

Tohorā southern right whale in Island Bay, offshore from the Marine Education Centre.

bay before heading west to Ōwhiro Bay and then out past Pariwhero Red Rocks on 15 July 2015 came right into the Siren Rocks lagoon.

Tohorā southern right whales were seen in Island Bay in July 2023 and December 2005, and there are resident parāoa sperm whales in Te Moana-o-Raukawa Cook Strait area, so a few are occasionally seen from the coast passing offshore.

Every year in May–July, paikea humpback whales migrate from Antarctic waters north through Te Moana-o-Raukawa area to tropical waters further north. One was seen off Island Bay on 23 July 2021, and two were seen breaching on 8 June 2020 about 500 metres off the south coast. On 6 May 2023 one was seen breaching just east of Taputeranga Island, and a larger one was seen swimming past Island Bay and Ōwhiro Bay four days later.

A rare Arnoux's beaked whale was seen repeatedly breaching off Island Bay on 8 January 2019. Six beaked whale species have been recorded stranded on the coastline of Te Whanganui-a-Tara: Arnoux's, Cuvier's, Andrew's, Gray's, Hector's and strap-toothed. Other strandings have included blue, pygmy right and pygmy sperm whales.

Siren Rocks to Ōwhiro Bay

From the path between Siren Rocks and Ōwhiro Bay keep an eye out for the bright orange pepe para riki coastal copper butterfly flitting around, and the orange-chequered, golden-brown wings of the forest glade butterfly in summer. Despite their vivid colours and painterly patterns, male and female butterflies mainly find each other by smell. Perhaps more than any other group, they illustrate how fascinating and beautiful insect life can be.

Male pepe para riki copper butterfly on ice plant flower.

Ōwhiro Stream flows into the sea at the northern end of Ōwhiro Bay's sandy beach, where flocks of karoro southern black-backed gulls and tarāpunga red-billed gulls gather with tōrea pango variable oystercatchers and kawau shags. Although still relatively abundant here on the south coast, the tarāpunga has suffered a marked decline at its largest breeding colonies elsewhere since the 1990s and it is now listed as an 'at risk – declining' species.

Two separate rāpoka leopard seals hauled out on Ōwhiro Bay beach on 10 October 2017 and 18–19 September 2021, both attracting wildlife-watchers and photographers before they swam back out to sea.

Following the path to the west end of Ōwhiro Bay Road, you arrive at Te Kopahou Reserve visitor centre car park, which is a popular nightspot for stargazers and astro-photographers because the night view to the south is unpolluted by city lights. Check out the Milky Way from here with binoculars or a telescope. Once in a blue moon you might even see a southern aurora, like the pink ones seen by aurora chasers from here on 24 April 2023 and 12 May 2024. Check the Aurora Australis (New Zealand) Facebook group for tips on when to go there.

GETTING THERE

Buses run regularly from the city to Island Bay (1, 32X), Ōwhiro Bay (29) and Houghton Bay (23), and there is a handy cycleway in Island Bay. There are parking areas near each of the bays, Te Raekaihau Point and the visitor centre.

View east from Hawkins Hill.

12 TE KOPAHOU RESERVE INCLUDING SPOOKY GULLY

Wild and windy Te Kopahou, a 600-hectare reserve in the steep hill country on the south coast of Te Upoko-o-te-Ika, supports a mosaic of regenerating native forest and shrubland habitats, and two streams, Waipapa and Te Haape. There are breathtaking views from its highest ridges across to the Kaikōura Ranges in Te Waipounamu South Island.

Te Kopahou Reserve is part of a wider area earmarked for the return of an important taonga bird species known in te ao Māori as te manu huna a Tāne, or 'the hidden bird of Tāne'. This is, of course, the kiwi.

Pariwhero Red Rocks Scientific Reserve and Te Rimurapa Sinclair Head are adjacent to the reserve on the coast, the latter being an important winter haul-out site for kekeno New Zealand fur seals.

Te Kopahou is located within a 23,000-hectare wider network of 4500 traps targeting invasive stoats and rats, which has been operational between Porirua and Pariwhero Red Rocks since 2020. After an absence of about 100 years from this part of the motu, 63 kiwi-nui North Island brown kiwi were released into the wild in a predator-free area in the hills above Mākara by the Capital Kiwi Project in 2022–23.

The releases at Terawhiti Station were part of the project's aim to 'restore a large-scale wild kiwi population to Wellington's backyard'. The 63 kiwi-nui were the first of 250 set to be released over five years. One of the radio-tracked birds was found above Karori on the Skyline Walkway in August 2023, and then in November that year two healthy chicks were found in a burrow near Mākara, the first hatched in the wild west of the capital for at least 100 years. The hope is that as this new population increases, birds will spread out to Te Kopahou Reserve and start breeding here as well.

Rimuroa violet harebell *(Wahlenbergia violacea)* flower.

Woollyhead flower.

The Capital Kiwi Project is a partnership between private landowners, community, tangata whenua, Wellington city and regional councils, Predator Free 2050 Ltd, the Department of Conservation, the Wellington Community Trust and a range of private philanthropists and donors. The project says that it had an initial focus in the south-west, where Taranaki Whānui ki Te Upoko o Te Ika has been a key partner since the project started, and that '[as] traps are deployed further north in the project area, a relationship is being forged with iwi mana whenua there: Ngāti Toa'.

The project also says that 'as kaitiaki, iwi are actively engaged in the mahi from trapping and monitoring [to] sharing knowledge, educating tamariki, representing and advocating for the project and as members of the project team, including building relationships with iwi who are the kaitiaki of kiwi at their source sites'.

Other native birds to watch for are pīhoihoi New Zealand pipits on the tracks, kārearea New Zealand falcons zooming overhead, kāhu swamp harriers gliding over the ridges, and both riroriro grey warblers and tauhou silvereyes in the scrub.

The gated 3.5-kilometre road connecting the Brooklyn wind turbine with Hawkins Hill has a wonderful abundance of ferns growing in the adjacent area, most of which are common species, but you may also find the scarce fine-leaved parsley fern. At 495 metres, Hawkins Hill is the highest point in the capital. In summer, the koromiko hebe flowering along here attract kahukura red admiral butterflies, and the rimuroa violet harebells (*Wahlenbergia violacea*) flowering on the verges attract pepe para riki copper butterflies. You can walk along the narrow Barking Emu Track, which runs parallel to and just below the road, and is a fairly even 45-minute walk to Hawkins Hill.

Being close to the south end of Zealandia, birds sometimes seen flying here include tūī, kererū New Zealand pigeon and kākā. The roadside banks and verges have a fascinating variety of upland plants, from taramea speargrass, tūtūmako North Island eyebright and white mountain violet to white-flowering alpine cranesbill, white-flowering rock harebell (*W. pygmaea*) and yellow-flowering woollyhead.

Tūtūmako grows up to 60 centimetres high and produces beautiful displays of its purple-striped white-and-yellow flowers in January–March. There is also red-and-white fruiting tāwiniwini snowberry and orange fruiting pātōtara dwarf mingimingi. Ground-hugging tiny filmy ferns, korokio mountain hard fern and ring fern are quite abundant in places, and there is alpine hard fern and a good variety of spleenwort ferns.

The two main tracks through the

The pepe para riki copper butterfly is common in mid-summer in warm, open places.

Mōkarakara magpie moth on koromiko hebe flower.

The long, narrow fronds of alpine hard fern.

Korokio mountain hard fern.

The lacy ring fern grows yellow-green fronds that have a distinctive smell in summer.

The kahukura red admiral butterfly is perhaps our most iconic butterfly.

reserve are demanding, with steep, rough uphill and downhill sections. From Hawkins Hill you can walk the Radome Track south towards the coast. Where it meets the Waipapa Loop Track, turn east onto a short track section until it meets the Red Rocks Track, and then turn west and follow the track south until it reaches the coast by Waipapa Stream between Pariwhero Red Rocks and Te Rimurapa Sinclair Head. This is about a 4-kilometre walk. Alternatively, you can walk the length of the Pariwhero Red Rocks Track from the top of the Tip Track, which runs along Spooky Gully and then rather steeply up and down until you reach the coast where the Waipapa Stream flows into the sea. This too is about a 4-kilometre walk. Both are demanding walks of 2–3 hours depending on the pace you set.

Spooky Gully is a distinct area within the north-east part of the reserve. It has closed-canopy koromiko hebe shrubland dominated by *Veronica parviflora*, a spreading tree with narrow leaves and white flower spikes that grows up to 7.5 metres tall. This habitat also has some attractive vines growing in it, including pōānanga Forster's clematis and tātarāmoa bush lawyer, which produces orange-red summer fruits shaped like small blackberries.

Te Kopahou Reserve has a patchwork of coastal grey-green scrub, flaxland, māhoe scrub and shrubland including wharariki coastal flax, ngaio, coastal tree daisy, wī silver tussock and īnanga needle-leaf grass tree. On the coast, it also has the white-flowering mat daisy *Raoulia glabra* and golden scabweed *R. australis*, both close relatives of the 'vegetable sheep' species. Some of the scarcer species in the reserve include small-leaved kōwhai, Cook Strait kōwhai and Cook Strait māhoe.

The endemic Cook Strait coastal bluebell (*Wahlenbergia ramosa*) produces its violet-white flowers in summer along some of the tracks to the south, and the scarce native slender greenhood orchid has been reported flowering near Te Kopahou trig during October.

Despite the drier summer climate, there is a good diversity of fern species in the reserve including small kiokio, shaking brake fern, butterfly fern and the regionally rare rock fern. The locally rare bristly cloak fern is known from only one site here. Among the diversity of winged insect life here, look out for the mōkarakara New Zealand magpie moth, kapokapowai New Zealand bush giant dragonfly and māwhitiwhiti migratory locust.

Māwhitiwhiti migratory locust laying an egg.

GETTING THERE

The routes of the number 7, 17 and 25 buses pass closest to the Brooklyn wind turbine. The number 29 bus stops in Ōwhiro Bay if you opt to walk back from Pariwhero Red Rocks or Te Rimurapa Sinclair Head via the coastal track and road. There is no public vehicle access past the Brooklyn wind turbine car park.

Tūtūmako North Island eyebright.

Īnanga needle-leaf grass tree near Hawkins Hill.

Īnanga *Dracophyllum* flowers.

View north up Te Haape Stream valley.

13 TE HAAPE STREAM VALLEY

Te Haape Stream flows 3 kilometres from Spooky Gully down through Te Kopahou Reserve, reaching the sea by the start of the 4WD track just past Te Kopahou visitor centre. It is about a 400-metre walk up this stream valley to a small waterfall if you want to explore this hidden gem. The valley is quite narrow in parts, but there is more to see here than at first glance.

Look out for the pīhoihoi New Zealand pipit flicking its long tail.

At the start you need to cross Te Haape Stream and walk upstream along the left bank for about 30 metres, then cross again to the right-hand bank via a stepping stone where the stream narrows. Do not walk up the extremely steep gravel track that veers off to the left of the stream (which goes up above the disused Ōwhiro quarry). Walking along the track on the right-hand bank is an easier way to access the interior of Te Kopahou Reserve than the longer inland tracks described in the previous chapter. As you walk further upstream, the more it feels like a 'hidden valley', and it is along here that you can find some interesting native plants and ferns growing by this burbling freshwater stream.

Starting where the stream reaches the sea, watch for any herons hunting with their long spear bill for small fish in the shallows. The streamlined warou welcome swallow can often be seen flying over the lower end of the stream on warm summer days. This is one of the most elegant birds. As it darts around over the water on predatory sorties you can usually see its orange-red face and throat, and the metallic blue lustre on its back and upper wings.

The more camouflaged pīhoihoi New Zealand pipit prefers standing on rocks near the start of the stream valley. This slender songbird in the wagtail family has a streaky front, pale eye stripes, and long legs. Watch for one flicking its long

Kihikihi wawā chirping cicada.

Cook Strait coastal bluebell.

The warou welcome swallow is one of our most elegant native birds.

tail while standing on a rock and listen for its slurry *tzweep* call, which is loud enough to carry up the valley.

Although not numerous here, a few maikaika common onion orchids and maikuku common sun orchids sometimes grow by a damp boggy patch not far from the start of the track, flowering in November–December. Further up the track you may also see some silver-back spider orchids and tutukiwi common greenhood orchids.

Rauhuia, the native flax linen, is quite abundant in the first 200 metres, with its delicate porcelain-white summer flowers, and the dainty white-flowering snowdrop wood-sorrel blooms here in summer. Two rather eye-catching native flowering plants in the valley are the Cook Strait coastal bluebell *Wahlenbergia ramosa*, which grows alongside the stream and flowers from about October to April, and the mountain daisy *Brachyglottis lagopus*, which produces its bright yellow flowers in December–January.

There is an impressively large piripiri pygmy tree orchid growing on rocks along the track. When this area was still forested, this species would have grown on the tall trunks of the rimu and northern rātā that towered over a canopy of tawa and kohekohe.

More colourful is the magenta-purple flowering naturally occurring native fuchsia hybrid, *F. excorticata* x *F. perscandens*. The small, yellow-flowering bachelor's button daisy and yellow and white flowering papatāniwhaniwha grow in the stream's splash zone. Giant tussock grasses of toetoe can be seen growing along here, as well as taramea speargrass, which produces its tall spiky flower stalks in spring and summer.

Watch out for the subtle pinātoro New Zealand daphne, which has many small creamy white flowers in summer, and its companion endemic orange-and-black geometrid day moth species, *Orocrambus fugitivellus*. There is also koromiko tree hebe, ongaonga stinging nettle and yellow-flowering *Leptinella squalida*.

The diversity of smaller ground ferns near the stream highlights how they can thrive in moist conditions. These include swamp kiokio palm-leaf fern, shore hard fern, pākau gully fern, rereti lance fern and a few puhinui Cunningham's maidenhair ferns.

The running water makes for some interesting insect life, foremost being the kapokapowai New Zealand bush giant dragonfly, an aerial predator from an ancient insect lineage that patrols over the stream in summer and swoops down to catch unsuspecting kihikihi cicadas. That's bad news for the cicada because they live for only a few weeks as winged adults after a couple of years as nymphs underground. Listen out too for male kihikihi wawā chirping cicadas singing in summer, one of about 50 endemic kihikihi cicada species in Aotearoa.

THE SOUTH COAST

Mountain daisy flowering.

Ongaonga stinging nettle.

Rauhuia flower.

Snowdrop wood-sorrel.

Piripiri pygmy tree orchid.

Shore hard fern.

Toetoe.

Te Haape Stream.

The summer butterflies to expect around here are pepe para riki North Island coastal coppers and both the kahukōwhai yellow admiral and kahukura red admiral. Also keep an eye out for the whē New Zealand mantis and kiki pounamu common katydid lurking in some of the streamside plants.

Although 400 metres is not far, the going can be quite slow as you navigate the rock clefts and stream boulders while progressing upstream. The unsealed track that runs alongside the stream is quite narrow and includes some sections with wet stepping stones and a few in-stream boulders that you need to scramble over. These may be slippery, so sturdy waterproof footwear is advisable. The water level and flow rate can vary, which can sometimes make it difficult to reach the waterfall.

GETTING THERE

The nearest bus is the number 29, which stops in Ōwhiro Bay, and you can find parking and some bike racks at the nearby Pariwhero Red Rocks visitor centre.

View west to Pariwhero Red Rocks.

14 PARIWHERO RED ROCKS SCIENTIFIC RESERVE
and Te Rimurapa Sinclair Head

This quintessential wilderness coastal walk along the southern section of Te Kopahou Reserve takes you to Pariwhero Red Rocks Scientific Reserve and Te Rimurapa Sinclair Head, where kekeno New Zealand fur seals haul out in winter. From the beaches, you can enjoy the superb view 120 kilometres across to the Kaikōura Ranges in Te Waipounamu South Island on clear days.

Just after the visitor centre car park and Te Haape Stream outlet you pass an extended raised ledge area to the right of the track. Here there is a colourful diversity of summer butterflies, such as flaming orange pepe para riki coppers, purplish-blue pepe ao uri common blues, and the kahukōwhai yellow and kahukura red admirals. It is worth pausing here to watch them nectaring on small flowers and appreciate their fragile fleeting beauty, which is a sublime embodiment of summer.

About 80 metres past the stream outlet by the main track you can see the ground-hugging pale green mat daisy *Raoulia hookerii*, a close relative of the endemic 'vegetable sheep' species, which produces tiny pixel-like yellow flowers in summer. Yellow-flowering sand buttercups, wī silver tussock and horokaka New Zealand ice plant also grow along here among the abundant wharariki coastal flax.

The coastal cliffs and escarpments between Ōwhiro Bay and Te Rimurapa that rise steeply 100–280 metres above sea level are covered in wharariki and grey-green scrub. Watch up these escarpments for the kāhu swamp harrier or kārearea New Zealand falcon in flight, and for tūī and tauhou silvereyes feeding on wharariki nectar. The calls of the tūī make for a sublime 'livecast' as you walk along the beach.

The distinctive plant communities along this part of the coast include

Taramea speargrass growing on scree slope.

over 100 species, many of which are threatened. The main habitat types here are tauhinu cottonwood, koromiko and māhoe scrub, and tussocklands. The widespread grey-green scrub has many small-leaved shrubs with fine, right-angled woody branches and a tangled appearance, such as mingimingi and takupurenga coastal tree daisy. Taramea speargrass and large-leaved pōhuehue have also colonised the gravel screes, while on the exposed tops, tussocks provide a habitat for the rare flightless Hutton's speargrass weevil, mokomoko northern grass skink and minimac gecko.

After about 2.5 kilometres you reach Pariwhero, which is a nationally important site of scientific significance with rocks dating from the earliest stages of the formation of Aotearoa. Brick-red siltstone is the most common red rock here, and there are pillow-shaped purple-red basalt lava rocks that formed during an underwater eruption. The hard red and pinkish-white chert rocks here are 250 million years old, among the oldest rocks in Te Ika-a-Māui North Island.

After Pariwhero you can make an optional short detour along the first few hundred metres of track by Waipapa Stream, which flows down to the sea between Pariwhero and Te Rimurapa. In summer there are māwhitiwhiti migratory locusts and kihikihi cicadas here. Mokomoko northern grass skinks often bask among the jumbled rocky area that rises from the stream up the eastern side of the valley, and there are some interesting plants to look for, such as leafless clematis and the regionally uncommon rock fern.

Minimac gecko.

A few hundred metres past the Waipapa Stream outlet you reach the winter kekeno haul-out at Te Rimurapa where over a hundred males regularly rest on coastal rocks from May to September after breeding in Te Waipounamu. Their grey-brown fur, long whiskers, pointed nose, external ears, and hind flippers that rotate forward distinguish them from other seal and sea lion species. Be careful not to get too close to them here as they can get grumpy, and their powerful bite contains infectious bacteria that can cause a serious, even fatal infection. Bull males can grow up to 2 metres long and weigh up to 250 kilograms. You can see them resting on the coastal rocks here just before and after the 'Devil's Gate' cutting through the headland, or as they swim around just offshore among the rimurapa bull kelp.

Sharp-eyed observers may also spy a pod of aihe dolphins passing offshore in summer, or a pod of maki orca. A pod of five maki were seen swimming west towards Pariwhero on 30 May 2023, a pod of four were seen between the visitor centre car park and Pariwhero on 24–25 October 2022, another pod of four were seen off Te Rimurapa on 13 August 2018, and two were seen between the car park and Pariwhero on 3 March 2018.

Te Papa vertebrates curator Alan Tennyson and naturalist Peter Langlands saw two tohorā blue whales from the Cook Strait ferry about 2 kilometres offshore from Pariwhero, heading east on 20 March

View of Pariwhero Red Rocks.

THE SOUTH COAST

Adult and juvenile tōrea pango variable oystercatchers.

Kekeno New Zealand fur seal winter haul-out.

Kekeno New Zealand fur seal yawning.

2019. The largest animal on Earth, these ocean giants grow up to 30 metres long and weigh up to 200 tonnes. The two they saw were probably migrating north from their Antarctic summer feeding grounds, possibly to a known blue whale wintering area off the Taranaki coast. Two were also filmed swimming off the south coast on 11 June 2023, and others were seen off the coast between Mākara and Mana on 31 January 2023, and Pukerua Bay on 9 April 2010. There are undated records of dead tohorā puru just past Karori lighthouse and just north of Mākara. One also washed up on the Kapiti Coast at Hokio Beach on 12 September 2023.

Three parāoa sperm whales were seen about 500 metres off Pariwhero on 7 December 2014, and a paikea humpback whale was seen breaching a few hundred metres off Te Kopahou visitor centre on 5 November 2013. A rare Shepherd's beaked whale stranded on the beach in Ōteranga Bay a few kilometres past Pariwhero in September 1998. Another rare local find was the Pacific olive ridley turtle found freshly dead near Te Rimurapa, reported on 18 October 2019. Apparently it had been run over by a vehicle.

The main resident birds are pīhoihoi New Zealand pipits, tōrea pango variable oystercatchers, tarāpunga red-billed gulls and karoro southern black-backed gulls. Matuku moana reef heron and white-faced heron also forage in the vicinity, so watch out for them stalking the shallows or flying along the coast. The area just past the 'Devil's Gate' by the seal haul-out has views across to Te Waipounamu, and pelagic seabirds can sometimes be seen passing offshore. Be sure to stand to one side of the track to avoid trail bikes and 4WD vehicles during days when the locked vehicle access gate is open.

A very rare and ecologically unique high-tide species of sea slug dubbed the 'Smeagol gravel maggot' also occurs in the vicinity!

GETTING THERE/AROUND

This walk follows the coastal 4WD track 4 kilometres west from Te Kopahou visitor centre at the end of Ōwhiro Bay Road. Be alert for vehicles and trail bikes using it. It takes about 45 minutes to walk to Pariwhero Red Rocks and another 15 minutes to Te Rimupara. It is also possible to cycle out with a few short interludes where you need to wheel your mountain bike across soft sand. The number 29 bus stops in Ōwhiro Bay and there is parking at the visitor centre. The metal gate at the start of the track is locked on Sundays. Please note all dogs must be kept on a leash.

View of Te Rae-akiaki Pencarrow Head and lighthouses.

15 TE MOANA-O-RAUKAWA COOK STRAIT FERRY

This iconic ferry journey, taking in Te Whanganui-a-Tara Wellington Harbour, Te Rae-akiaki Pencarrow Head, the south coast and Te Moana-o-Raukawa Cook Strait, offers a unique perspective on wild Wellington whether you're arriving or departing. It is also a great opportunity to see majestic pelagic seabirds and aihe dolphins from the deck.

A ferry crossing to or from Te Waipounamu South Island can be a good way to see pelagic seabirds such as toroa albatrosses, tāiko petrels and tītī shearwaters. Pods of aihe common dolphins sometimes follow in the ferry's wake or surf the bow wave, and maki orca are also possible. So, too, are tohorā puru blue whales, as mentioned in the previous chapter.

Paikea humpback, parāoa sperm and tohorā southern right whales may be seen here, especially during their northern migration from Antarctica to tropical waters in late autumn and early winter. Te Moana-o-Raukawa is where the first deep-water orange roughy were caught by Victoria University of Wellington researchers who were trying to catch one of the wheke nui giant squid that parāoa feed on, and the hoki that spawn here are an important food source for kekeno New Zealand fur seals.

Strong westerlies sometimes blow through the strait, so be prepared for a windy and wet crossing with plenty of swell; but it can also be fairly calm, which is good for spotting dolphins or whales at the surface. Binoculars can help if you want to stand on deck and watch for seabirds following the ferry. It's also worth pausing to take in the wild seascape and cloud formations. Thunderstorms with lightning occasionally pass over Cook Strait.

Good numbers of seabirds are sometimes seen streaming through the

Female toroa Antipodean albatross.

strait. The toroa albatross species to watch for are white-capped, black-browed, Salvin's, Buller's, northern royal, southern royal, Antipodean, wandering and light-mantled sooty. The last is an especially sought-after species for birdwatchers. It is a relatively small, dark chocolate-brown albatross with a silvery grey mantle and back, pointed wings and tail, and a black bill with a blue stripe.

Toroa albatross are the ultimate avian windsurfers, riding stormy winds over long distances on weeks-long trips that can cover thousands of kilometres, during which they feed on squid and fish to take back to their growing chick at the nest.

Toroa northern royal albatross.

Pāngurunguru northern giant petrel.

Toroa southern royal albatross.

Toroa Salvin's albatross.

Toroa pango light-mantled sooty albatross.

Toroa black-browed albatross.

During a lifetime a single toroa can fly over 8.5 million kilometres, equivalent to more than ten times the distance from Earth to the Moon and back.

At over 3 metres, wandering and royal albatrosses have the largest wingspan of all seabirds and can weigh up to 10 kilograms, or about the same weight as a newborn dolphin. Between them, the different toroa species muster a wide range of bill colours, from pink or bluish-grey to yellow with an orange tip, or black with a blue stripe. They use the razor-sharp bill to slice up squid and fish – and to threaten other toroa when they squabble over food.

The other seabirds to watch for are pāngurunguru giant petrels, Westland and karetai kauae mā white-chinned tāiko petrels, pakahā fluttering and Hutton's tītī shearwaters, karetai hurukoko Cape petrels and tītī wainui fairy prions. Subantarctic-breeding species such as soft-plumaged petrels and white-headed petrels are sometimes seen in winter, and a very rare sighting was a south polar skua seen from a ferry crossing the strait on 19 January 2013. Tara white-fronted terns and tarāpunga red-billed gulls are also seen regularly, and a few tarapirohe black-fronted terns cross the strait in autumn and spring on their annual migrations.

On the return journey be sure not to miss the views as the ferry passes Te Rae-akiaki Pencarrow Head into Te Whanganui-a-Tara Wellington Harbour,

Karetai kauae mā white-chinned petrel.

then past Matiu Somes Island and across to the ferry terminal near the city. On a clear day the views seem endless.

GETTING THERE

Ferries depart from the Wellington ferry terminal to Waitohi Picton several times a day on their return trips. The number 83 bus route from the Wellington central bus station and from Hutt city centre passes close to the Cook Strait ferry terminals at Waterloo Quay. There is also parking nearby.

Maki orca and toroa albatrosses seen on the way out to Nicholson Canyon.

16 NICHOLSON CANYON AND COOK CANYON PELAGIC SEABIRDS

A pelagic seabird watching trip from Te Whanganui-a-Tara Wellington Harbour out to the waters above the impressively deep Nicholson Canyon and Cook Canyon is an unforgettable way to experience close encounters with majestic toroa albatrosses and pāngurunguru giant petrels at sea off the south coast. In te ao Māori, this is the realm of Tangaroa.

Since 2016, Te Whanganui-a-Tara branch of Birds New Zealand has been organising trips from Seaview marina with Cook Strait Charters skipper Jonathan Delich to see the diverse range of pelagic seabirds found off the south coast over the nearest underwater canyons.

Although these trips sometimes have to be cancelled due to rough sea conditions, when they go ahead they have an excellent track record of seeing toroa albatrosses close-up in good numbers over waters that are 400–600 metres deep. On one of the first trips in May 2016 we saw hundreds of individual toroa near the boat, among which we recorded eight species: a rare Tasmanian shy albatross, plus northern and southern royals, Antipodean, Buller's, Salvin's, black-browed and white-capped albatross. Most were sitting on the water as a nearby trawler hauled in its nets. Our skipper positioned his boat well away to the side and we watched as toroa glided effortlessly around us before landing on the water using their pink-webbed feet as landing 'skis'.

A more recent highlight was an August 2023 trip when we had a very close encounter with a pod of three maki orca swimming around the boat about 8 kilometres offshore over Nicholson Canyon, where the water depth is about 400 metres. They turned on their monochrome magic for us: at one point, the big bull brought a hāpuku grouper to the surface, which one of the younger maki came over to feed on, also attracting toroa and karetai hurukoko Cape petrels. That day, we also recorded the first sighting of a rare Antarctic fulmar on one of these trips, as it flew in and joined the flock of karetai hurukoko on the water. We also recorded six toroa species, which is not unusual for these trips.

The seabird species seen usually depends on the time of year. Northern and southern pāngurunguru giant petrels, karetai hurukoko Cape petrels, tītī wainui fairy prions and pakahā

Pāngurunguru southern giant petrel.

Karetai hurukoko Cape petrel.

Toroa northern royal albatross landing on the water.

fluttering shearwaters tend to be seen year-round. Rako Buller's shearwaters, tītī sooty shearwaters, toanui flesh-footed shearwaters, Arctic skuas and tara white-fronted terns are more often seen in the warmer months, while tarapirohe black-fronted terns, tāiko Westland petrels and karetai kauae mā white-chinned petrels are more often seen in the colder months. Short-tailed shearwaters have been seen during May–November, while a few other species, such as tītī Cook's petrel, kuaka common diving petrel and takahikare white-faced storm petrel, are less predictable.

The larger species make marathon annual migrations. For example, tītī sooty shearwaters breed at the Foveaux Islands and Mauka Huka the Subantarctic Islands from September to May before their annual migration across Te Moana-Nui-a-Kiwa Pacific Ocean to waters off Japan, Alaska and California, returning to Aotearoa the following September.

When seabirds come in and land on the water near the boat it is an opportunity to see them at close range and take photographs. The wilderness experience is completed by the toroa making a cacophony of braying and snorting calls as they quarrel over the pecking order. A scrum of toroa and pāngurunguru

Toroa Buller's albatross (front) and toroa black-browed albatross.

Toroa white-capped albatross.

Toroa southern royal and Buller's albatross with karetai hurukoko Cape petrel.

Toroa royal and Buller's albatross scrum with karetai hurukoko Cape petrels.

Antarctic fulmar, a winter visitor to Te Moana-o-Raukawa Cook Strait.

Tītī wainui fairy prion.

The tākapu Australasian gannet is a temperate-water relative of the tropical boobies.

squabbling over fish scraps is something you won't soon forget.

We also often enjoy close views of aihe common dolphins, and a pod of streamlined, silvery dusky dolphins – a short-beaked native species with a patchy circumpolar distribution – sometimes comes in to ride the bow wave.

Parāoa sperm whales have also been seen out over the underwater canyons, where they can dive deep to catch wheke nui giant squid. The wheke nui is a true giant of the ocean, growing up to 13 metres with tentacles up to 10 metres long and weighing up to 275 kilograms. Common in Te Moana-o-Raukawa Cook Strait, they also sometimes wash up on south coast beaches.

Parāoa is the largest of all toothed whale species and the largest toothed predator in the world. This marine apex predator has the largest brain of any animal and can live for up to 70 years. Males can grow up to 24 metres long and weigh up to 80 tonnes, and they have been recorded diving down over 2000 metres and staying underwater for an hour and fifty minutes. During a trip out to Nicholson Canyon on 6 November 2022, we observed a huge parāoa bursting up out of the water like a submarine as it surfaced about a kilometre from the boat.

The toroa and pāngurunguru seen out here are on foraging trips from their breeding grounds at Mauka Huka the Subantarctic Islands or Rēkohu Chatham Islands, or dispersing after breeding or fledging. Black-browed albatross come here in winter from their South Atlantic breeding sites, while the smaller seabirds are from closer breeding sites, such as Matiu Somes Island, Mana Island, Kapiti Island or islands in the Marlborough Sounds.

It is fascinating to watch the feeding techniques of the different seabird species. Toroa mainly grab food off or near the surface – or from each other! Karetai hurukoko Cape petrels sieve tiny particles of food from the surface. Storm petrels glide and dance over the water, grabbing at tiny particles of food. Some tītī shearwaters and tāiko petrels use a technique called snorkelling, swimming along the surface with their head and neck submerged and their wings raised to help steer and propel themselves. Some also dive underwater and use their wings to propel themselves in pursuit of small fish.

Tara terns hover a few metres over the water and plunge or dip down to grab small food items off the surface. The much larger tākapu Australasian gannet can dive like an arrow from up to 30 metres in the air, hitting the water at about 100 kilometres per hour and plunging down a few metres. It can then 'fly' underwater using wings and feet to propel itself in pursuit of fish, going down as deep as 30 metres.

Kororā little blue penguins are mostly seen swimming at the surface in the harbour, looking around as the boat passes them. They can also 'fly' underwater propelled by their flippers and feet to chase after small fish as deep as 60 metres.

If you join one of these trips it is advisable to bring waterproofs, wear sturdy footwear and take seasickness medication if you need it. Lunch and lifejackets are provided.

GETTING THERE

Twenty places on each trip are offered to Birds New Zealand members in advance via email. Any spaces left unfilled the week before the trip are notified to non-members via the New Zealand Birders Facebook group on a first come, first served basis. These share-cost trips usually depart from Seaview Marina at 7am for 6–9 hours. The number 81 and 83 buses run close to Seaview Marina from Wellington central bus station and Queensgate in Lower Hutt, and there is parking at the marina. The pier and the boat have wheelchair access.

TE AWA KAIRANGI
THE HUTT VALLEY

Te mākurukuru o Te Awa Kairangi: The profuse abundance of the Hutt Valley	142
17. Korokoro Dam Loop Track, in Belmont Regional Park	146
18. Pito One Beach and Te Awa Kairangi Hutt River mouth	152
19. Matiu Somes Island scientific and historic reserve	158
20. East Harbour Regional Park northern forest including Ōtuamotoro, Muritai and Butterfly Creek	164
21. Parangarahu Lakes at Te Rae-akiaki	186
22. Puketahā forest in Wainuiomata Mainland Island	192
23. Percy Scenic Reserve and alpine plant collection	200
24. Kaitoke Regional Park swingbridge track circuit	206

TE MĀKURUKURU O TE AWA KAIRANGI: THE PROFUSE ABUNDANCE OF THE HUTT VALLEY

Liz Mellish MNZM, Amokura, Te Wharewaka o Pōneke

The beautiful valley of Te Awa Kairangi used to be a podocarp forest with many streams and rivers that traversed the valley floor, home to many species of birds, insects and freshwater fish. The valley was navigable up to Kaitoke and the Waiwhetū Stream to present-day Silverstream. The valley teemed with mahinga kai food resources and rongoā medicinal plants, all the necessary requirements for life.

The wonderful nīkau and kahikatea predominated and there are still remnants of the original forests to explore. The ngahere forest included rimu and tōtara, which were vital for building waka. Charles Heaphy wrote about the sight encountered by settlers on arrival into Te Whanganui-a-Tara of this forested valley, which was flat, but not cleared and ready to be farmed as they had been led to believe. Te Āti Awa allowed the settlers to use raupō to build houses as their first accommodation and supplied water and food under the direction of Hōniana Te Puni-kōkopu. Heaphy noted too that there were kererū in flocks numbering more than a thousand, easily shot and beautiful to eat. Food was plentiful – trees such as rimu have sweet berries, kareao supplejack has soft shoots which are also good to eat, and much more. It is interesting to see Māori chefs today around the country collecting and celebrating the fruits of the ngahere forest in their menus.

Mana whenua were provided with tuna eels in large quantities and the inner harbour was populated by pelagic fish, from whitebait to mullet, kahawai, and tuna at the delta of Te Awa Kairangi and Waiwhetū and their tributaries. What we called the summer papakāinga ancestral settlement extended from Waiwhetū Pā to Turakirae and were used in tune with the seasons. This allowed whānau access to their own fishing grounds, respecting the right of each other to harvest and provide manaakitanga for their manuhiri guests. Mana whenua could, and still can, collect shellfish at the appropriate times while attending to fishing regulations, which enables us to continue the practice of manaakitanga.

Whānau were able to practise essential arts and crafts, such as home-building, weaving clothing and teaching the skills necessary to survive in Te Whanganui-a-Tara. Harakeke flax was harvested for trade centred at Kumutoto Pā in Wellington City. Much of the cultivated harvest was gathered for sale to the new settlers in both Wellington and the Hutt Valley as the nation was established. The international trade, especially to New South Wales in Australia and Europe, came through Te Whanganui-a-Tara.

The journey through Te Awa Kairangi starts at Korokoro Dam Loop Track in Belmont Regional Park. The Korokoro Stream valley supports many plants used for rongoā. It was an easy place for whānau to gather what they needed to supply Pito One Pā and these days for Te Tatau o Te Pō marae on the old Hutt Road. Korokoro Stream has very pure water and is a good place to see native fish species, namely kōkopu of many varieties. It flows into the harbour at Hōniana Te Puni Reserve on the waterfront at Pito One Petone.

This neatly brings us to Pito One Petone Beach and its relationship with the mouth of Te Awa Kairangi, sometimes now known as the estuary. Pito One Beach begins at the southern entrance to the valley from Pōneke Wellington City, bounded by the Korokoro Stream. The following narrative by Matiu Jennings tells a story of this stream and its relationship to the harbour islands.

'Whātatitai [the taniwha] was washed down Te Korokoro-o-te-Ika (the throat of the fish), causing it to cough, and Whātaitai and three morsels flew out. The morsels became islands in the harbour, Matiu, Mākaro and Mokopuna, but Whātaitai was stranded and grew weak and died.'

The Hutt River mouth is an interactive tidal area full of life. The two pā that originally sat on either side of the river mouth, Waiwhetū Pā to the east and Hīkoikoi Pā to the west, were dramatically affected by settlement and the river constantly flooded. As the Harbour Board and Petone Council tried to mitigate flooding, a new relationship developed between the awa and the harbour. Dredging has meant that access to fish such as flounder, mullet, kahawai and conger eels has largely diminished. However, the Waione Street bridge, which fords the awa at the mouth, is crowded by fishermen catching food for their whānau most days. I believe they are successful as they return constantly. The shape of the river mouth has been modified, closing off traditional practices such as gathering fish, dyeing harakeke and launching waka, but the knowledge of what is possible is still there with various whānau retaining that knowledge.

As part of the Treaty of Waitangi settlement claims, Matiu Island is now owned by the Māori collective Taranaki Whānui ki Te Upoko o Te Ika and co-governed by the Department of Conservation (DOC) and Port Nicholson Block Settlement Trust. Matiu has tuatara roaming freely, and alongside the gecko and other lizards, their presence here is a tribute to the work done since the islands were managed by DOC. Many transfers of species have been facilitated by iwi and connected into other sanctuaries in Te Tauihu, Kapiti, Taranaki, Whanganui, Pūkaha and Cape Kidnappers. Matiu has predator-free status now, as over many years groups of volunteers have trapped and removed plant pests to allow the animals to roam freely. The island is also a sanctuary for kororā. It has a whare called Whare Mahana where iwi can stay overnight and experience the thrill of seeing the nightly return of up to 400 pairs of penguins, catch a peek of the elusive tuatara, enjoy the thrill of kākāriki dive-bombing in large groups and the occasional kārearea that come in from the Hutt Valley.

Continuing the journey around the east coast past Eastbourne you find the East Harbour Regional Park. This park includes former summer pā and has within it land still in the possession of whānau of Te Tatau o Te Pō. In early days, wheat was grown at Fitzroy Bay to supply settlers' flour mills located at Ngā Ūranga, Ngaio Gorge and Matairangi Mount Victoria in easy reach for traders. Fishing is good for kahawai, gurnard and sometimes kingfish. It is somewhat hampered by the Pencarrow outfall but as the treatment of sewage is improving the sea will recover a lot from the degradation. Whānau divers who know the places least affected by the sewage disposal are still able to access good shellfish. It is also open to access now from Wainuiomata at Baring Head, or, as we know it, Ōrua-pouanui, the marker signalling entry to Palliser Bay. Other notable places on our journey are Ōtuamotoro Days Bay, Muritai and Butterfly Creek, all areas where whānau have foraged and enjoyed the views across the harbour to Raukawa Moana and Kaikōura in Te Tauihu. Great walking but steep.

The Parangarahu Lakes just past the Pencarrow lighthouses were returned to Te Āti Awa, Taranaki Whānui as cultural redress and are now owned and managed by Port Nicholson Block Settlement Trust. These are lakes that have received little impact from human development so are wonderful barometers of the health of freshwater from the streams that flow into them. Being so close to the sea they are home to special bird species that we have always protected through rāhui regulations. Pohowera banded dotterels breed on the beach but are vulnerable to predators, especially humans. The lakes are home to native fish including tuna eels and many bird species.

Puketahā forest, the mainland island for Wainuiomata, is a great place to understand the forest world before human settlement. The forest is beautiful and contains many species of flora and fauna not seen in other places. Many volunteers have supported the removal of pests and we have been involved in advocating for the transformation to mainland island status.

Bordering State Highway 2, Percy Scenic Reserve has been in the kaitiakitanga of the whānau of Te Tatau o Te Pō since its inception, somewhat like Ōtari but possibly not as well known. This is a lovely place for whānau to meet with the ngahere and enjoy picnicking, with weddings often held here.

It is interesting that many of the wildlife location highlights in this book are water catchments that supply the three cities and Porirua with their drinking water supply. Kaitoke Regional Park is the main part of this supply chain, where the Pākuratahi River meets Te Awa Kairangi.

The few remnants of Te Āti Awa land here at Pākuratahi are part of the Wellington Tenths Māori land. This is one of the few remaining farms in Upper Hutt. The land on the western side of State Highway 2 was taken by the Crown for agri-research but the dairy farm is still operating.

Track entrance with signage.

17 KOROKORO DAM LOOP TRACK, BELMONT REGIONAL PARK

This tranquil, lush forested stream valley on the south-east side of Belmont Regional Park, nestled in the forested hills overlooking Lower Hutt, is one of a few wild places in the Pōneke area where it is possible to see both red-crowned and yellow-crowned kākāriki on the mainland.

These two dainty, long-tailed green parakeet species are closely related and look very similar. The red-crowned kākāriki is the larger of the two, growing up to 28 centimetres and weighing up to 80 grams; the slightly smaller yellow-crowned kākāriki grows up to 25 centimetres and weighs up to 50 grams. The red-crowned has a red patch of feathers above the bill that extends onto the crown and behind the eyes, while the yellow-crowned has a small red band of feathers above the bill with a larger patch of yellow feathers above it that extends onto the crown, and no red behind the eyes.

Red-crowned kākāriki.

Look out for them in flight, or perched in the forest feeding on berries, or, in the case of the red-crowned, standing on the track feeding on fallen seeds. Listen out for their chattering calls or their softer, quieter *tur-tur-tur* calls, which can help you locate them. They are often seen individually, but sometimes fly erratically in duos or trios.

Yellow-crowned kākāriki perched on coprosma.

Listed as 'at risk – declining', the yellow-crowned kākāriki was reintroduced to Mana Island in 2005–6, and the 'at risk – relict' red-crowned kākāriki was reintroduced to Matiu Somes Island in 2003–4. Both species are now spreading out to the adjacent mainland.

A bench lookout near the western start of the track overlooks the stream valley across to Belmont Regional Park, which is a good vantage point to watch for the kākāriki as well as kererū New Zealand pigeon, tūī and kārearea New Zealand falcon. Watch out also along the tracks for tūī singing from a perch, all fluffed up.

The two-hour loop track winds down from Oakleigh Street in the suburb of Korokoro into the stream valley with some steep sections in both directions, and can be walked clockwise or anticlockwise from the two different entrances near the Oakleigh Street parking area. The loop track is quite a shady native forest walk so is best explored during the warmer months at a time of day when the sun is higher in the sky.

Nīkau in fruit, the endemic palm tree of Aotearoa.

Male miromiro New Zealand tomtit.

Pīwakawaka New Zealand fantail, adult pied morph.

Pīwakawaka New Zealand fantail, adult dark morph.

THE HUTT VALLEY

Another native bird to look out for here is the lively little black-and-white miromiro New Zealand tomtit. In common with its larger relative, the toutouwai North Island robin, the male has a small white spot of feathers at the top of the base of the bill that it can enlarge during displays. Listen out for its short *seet, zet* or *swee* contact calls. Miromiro sometimes forage with mixed flocks of tauhou silvereye and riroriro grey warbler. If you see a small flock, it is worth pausing to watch them, and if you hear a miromiro nearby, wait a little longer because it might fly in and perch on a branch close to the track for a closer look at you.

The other more abundant bush birds in the park here are korimako bellbird, pōpokotea whitehead, pīwakawaka New Zealand fantail and, in spring and summer, the pīpīwharauroa shining cuckoo. The pīwakawaka is a chirpy small flycatcher with two colour morphs. The more common 'pied' morph is brown above and buff below with a grey head, white 'eyebrows' and a thin, dark collar. The scarce dark morph is all blackish-brown and sometimes has a pale spot behind each eye. As the name suggests, this bird fans its tail, a behaviour that helps it to disturb its small insect prey.

Korimako bellbirds are more often heard than seen, singing mainly at dawn and dusk. Their song varies by region and always includes chiming notes, but lacks any grunts or wheezes. They also have a rapidly repeated, harsh *yeng-yeng-yeng* alarm call. In contrast, the tūī has a more complex mix of tuneful notes punctuated with coughs, grunts and wheezes. In flight, tūī maintain audio contact with each other and can harass raptors with a repeated shrill scream. So if you hear their screams, look up and you might see them chasing a kārearea.

Kōtare sacred kingfishers, pūtangi-

Korimako bellbird (male), named for its song which was said to sound like small bells.

tangi paradise shelduck and pūkeko are sometimes seen near the dam, where there is also the possibility of a kapokapowai New Zealand bush giant dragonfly flying around hawking for pēpepe butterflies and kihikihi cicadas. Korokoro Stream has a few native freshwater fish species, mainly tuna short-finned eels and ōrea long-finned eels, but also red-finned and blue-gilled bullies. Cave wētā have also been reported lurking by the dam.

The forest here is mainly tawa, hīnau, kohekohe and rewarewa with some pukatea, nīkau and kawakawa. Kiekie, scarlet rātā vine and puawānanga native clematis sometimes grow near the track.

Among the native orchids, check along the track for green bird orchid in December, the maikuku common sun orchid and maikaika common onion orchid in November–December, the tutukiwi greenhood orchid in October–December and the perching raupeka Easter orchid in January–March.

The shady and moist location here helps make for a very good diversity of tree ferns including pākau gully fern mamaku black tree fern, ponga silver fern, kātote Smith's tree fern, pūnui slender tree fern and whekī rough tree fern. The ground ferns also put on a good show, with petako sickle spleenwort, wharengārara lance fern, raurenga kidney fern and fan-like filmy fern.

Mokomoko northern grass skink and glossy brown skink have been reported

Pākau gully fern.

in the vicinity, so keep an eye out for any basking where the sun beats down on the track. There are pepe para riki North Island coastal copper and kahukura red admiral butterflies in summer, and the cicadas here include April green and kihikihi lesser bronze.

A colourful variety of fungi grow by the track and on the steep bank cuttings mainly in autumn and winter, including lilac coral fungus, the pale bluish *Entoloma canoconicum*, the green verdigris waxcap, the red puapua-a-autahi anemone stinkhorn and orange waxgills.

GETTING THERE

The number 150 bus stops nearby on Oakleigh Street (both directions) and at Pito One Petone railway station, from where trains run regularly to Pōneke and Upper Hutt. There is parking at the end of Oakleigh Street, close to both entrances to the loop track.

Tara white-fronted tern flock with tarāpunga red-billed gulls on Pito One Petone wharf.

18 PITO ONE BEACH AND TE AWA KAIRANGI HUTT RIVER MOUTH

Te Awa Kairangi Hutt River flows down from the Tararua Range for more than 50 kilometres. The lower river has fast-flowing braided sections before it forms an estuary below Ava bridge and Waione Street bridge in Lower Hutt, and then widens to about 200 metres where it flows into Te Whanganui-a-Tara Wellington Harbour at the east end of Pito One Petone Beach.

A walk along the west side of the estuary and Pito One Petone Beach is a chance to see big skies and wide vistas across the harbour to Miramar Peninsula, Matiu Somes Island and the Remutaka Range.

At low tide the mudflats below Waione Street bridge attract waterfowl such as kakīānau black swans and pūtangitangi paradise shelducks, wading birds such as spur-winged plovers, poaka pied stilts and white-faced herons, and coastal seabirds such as tara white-fronted terns and tarāpunga red-billed gulls.

A few migrant waders also feed here between spring and autumn, including kuaka bar-tailed godwits. There are also a few records of matuku moana reef heron, pāteke brown teal and tarāpuka black-billed gull.

Kōtuku ngutupapa royal spoonbills have become more abundant here in recent years, so it's worth watching for them feeding in the shallows and roosting on the gravel bars, or at nearby Te Mome Stream alongside Shandon golf course.

A kōtuku white heron with a long yellow spear bill is sometimes seen at the boat sheds and nearby Hīkoikoi Reserve and Te Mome Stream on the west side of the estuary during April–June. This is a bird on migration from the only kōtuku breeding site in the country at Ōkarito Lagoon in Te Waipounamu South Island. After breeding they disperse, with some migrating north to Te Ika-a-Māui North Island for the winter.

Kōtuku white heron standing on a post.

Tōrea pango variable oystercatchers are common here, and smaller numbers of tōrea South Island pied oystercatchers visit the estuary and beach in July–November. There are three morphs of tōrea pango – black, intermediate and pied – hence the name variable. All adults have a long orange bill, chunky coral-red legs and red eyes. Pied tōrea pango can be separated from tōrea by having a smudgy border on the breast and shoulder 'tab'. All adult tōrea are pied with a sharp border on the breast, a long orange bill, red legs and red eyes.

A flock of tara frequently roosts on Pito One Petone wharf during the warmer

Tōrea South Island pied oystercatcher visiting Pōneke on its migration north.

A young taranui Caspian tern begging its parent for food.

The tarāpuka black-billed gull is named for its slender black bill.

months and forages offshore and along the estuary. These birds are sometimes joined by taranui Caspian terns and an occasional tarapirohe black-fronted tern in autumn. All five of Te Upoko-o-te-Ika's kawau shag species can sometimes be seen roosting on the jetty and feeding in the area. Flocks of up to 2000 pakahā fluttering shearwaters sometimes feed offshore in summer, attracting tara, kawau and tākapu Australasian gannets to join the feeding frenzy.

The quieter east end of the beach is an area where kekeno New Zealand fur seals sometimes haul out to nap in the sun. In recent years, a few Antarctic seal species have also been found resting on Pito One Petone Beach. The rāpoka leopard seals that hauled out on 8 September 2022 near the jetty and on 14 October 2018 near the Settlers Museum both attracted hundreds of seal-watchers to admire their huge jaws and canine teeth as they yawned between snoozes. These fearless 'ice leopards' can grow up to 3.5 metres long and weigh up to 600 kilograms; but make sure you stay at least 20 metres away as they can retract their large head and strike like a snake.

There is also a history of Antarctic crabeater seals turning up on Pito One Petone Beach, with sightings recorded on 15 June 1933, 6 July 1934 and 18 December

1963, and more recently on 6 April 2022 by the Settlers Museum. One also swam up the Hutt River during March 2015 before it was found dead 18 kilometres upstream and added to Te Papa's collection. There were also sightings at Shandon golf course on 15 June 1933 and Melling on 7 July 1934. Another was filmed swimming in Te Awa Kairangi on 29 July 2019 about 7 kilometres upstream.

Pods of maki orca visit the harbour to hunt for rays, sometimes with a calf. In 2023, December–January and May–July were productive periods, with weekly sightings of pods of maki, though most sightings in Pōneke from 2008 to 2023 were reported during the December–February period or the June–September period. In 2022, a pod of five was seen off Pito One Petone Beach on 27 October, a pod of three on 26 December and a pod of two on 20 August. Prior to that, various maki were seen four times between late 2009 and late 2019.

During early July 2018, the tohorā southern right whale known as Matariki swam along and breached off Pito One Petone Beach. Two paikea humpback whales were also seen swimming from Pito One Petone Beach towards Pōneke on 11 June 2023. A very rare pygmy right whale, the smallest of the baleen whale species, washed up dead on Pito One Petone Beach near the jetty on 27 August 2023.

Pods of aihe common dolphins are often seen passing off Pito One Petone Beach in summer. A more unusual find on the beach was a dead tutumairekurai Hector's dolphin that washed up in 1978. In January 2009 the first live one was reported off the beach. Several more sightings of the same dolphin were reported in the harbour during summer and autumn of 2009, including photos and footage. Then on 14 November 2011 another was seen off Māhanga Bay on Motu Kairangi Miramar Peninsula.

Tutumairekurai is the only endemic dolphin species in Aotearoa and the world's smallest dolphin. It is so small that an adult could fit into a bathtub! It is threatened with extinction, mainly due to drowning in set-nets.

The Pito One Petone foreshore has a shallow 3.5-kilometre sandy beach with dune vegetation including whararahi coastal flax, pink-flowering shore bindweed, strand sedge, and some plantings of nau Cook's scurvy grass and guano groundsel. In recent years the Friends of Petone Beach have been planting coastal species such as pīngao and kōwhangatara spinifex to help form sand dunes and working to get rid of invasive exotic dune species. The beach is also known for its glinting diversity of marine shells, including tiara top shell and pink top shell.

Rāpoka leopard seal on Pito One Petone Beach, 8 September 2022.

Mōkarakara magpie moth on pīngao.

Pīngao sand dune habitat.

THE HUTT VALLEY

GETTING THERE

Trains connect Pito One Petone station with Pōneke and Upper Hutt. The number 81, 84 and 130 buses stop at the railway station and have stops near the eastern end of Pito One Petone Beach. Bus numbers 81, 83, 84, 110 and 130 run along Jackson Street parallel with Pito One Beach, about 300 metres inland. There is parking along the Pito One foreshore, including by the Settlers Museum, and the paved area adjacent to the beach is bike friendly. During daylight saving, dogs are not allowed on Pito One Beach between 9am and 8pm; they must be on a leash at other times.

View of the north end of the island.

19 MATIU SOMES ISLAND
scientific and historic reserve

Like a giant shard of dark green pounamu framed by the silvery-green sea, the 24-hectare Matiu Somes Island lies about 3 kilometres south of Pito One Petone Beach. From its elevated tracks and ridges there are big views of the harbourside landscapes. This is a great place to see red-crowned kākāriki, tuatara, Cook Strait giant wētā, and various gecko and mokomoko skink species.

The best time to visit Matiu is during the warmer months. Ferries regularly depart from Queens Wharf on the 8-kilometre trip to the island. From the other direction it is 4 kilometres from Ōtuamotoro Days Bay Wharf to the island. On a still, clear day when the sea can be glassy smooth, the surface reflects the sky like a mirror and the blueness seems to stretch forever, above and below. These are perfect conditions to take the ferry and watch for kororā little blue penguins swimming at the surface. The ferry's engine prompts the kororā to surface and swim out of its way. The front and sides of the upper deck of the ferry are the best vantage points, and binoculars can help you find the birds anywhere from a few metres away to over 100 metres distant.

The ferry is also a good vantage point to spot aihe common dolphins or maki orca, or even a whale. A pod of five maki was seen from the ferry on 15 July 2023, and a pod of six was seen on 27 October 2022. Two adult maki with a calf were also seen swimming around the island on 20 December 2009. As the ferry gains speed, also watch for pakahā fluttering shearwaters feeding at the surface or flying alongside. These dark brown and white coastal seabirds, which breed at Matiu during September–February, have a distinctive 'flutter-glide' flight pattern.

Tara white-fronted terns sometimes feed with the pakahā, so watch for them hovering over the surface, as well as the

Pakahā fluttering shearwater.

tākapu Australasian gannets flying past in summer and Arctic skuas that come into the harbour from September to March. The Arctic skua is a strong-flying, piratical seabird with long-pointed wings and a scything, falcon-like flight. Dark adults are deep brown, pale adults have a brown back and mainly white underparts, and intermediate adults are dark with paler underparts, head and neck. All have white flashes near the wingtips. The skua breeds in Arctic Alaska during the northern summer, and then migrates across the Pacific Ocean to Aotearoa for the southern summer. It feeds by aggressively pursuing terns or gulls until they disgorge their food, and then catching the fish as it falls through the air.

Since the island was returned to Taranaki Whānui ki Te Upoko o Te Ika in a 2008 Treaty of Waitangi settlement it has been governed by the Matiu Somes

Tākapu Australasian gannet.

Arctic skua.

The ornate skink is named for its intricate markings.

Island Kaitiaki Board and managed by the Department of Conservation (DOC). After a short biosecurity briefing near the wharf, you are free to make your way around the island. On a warm, still day, you should see some of the resident red-crowned kākāriki that now breed here after successful translocations in 2003–4. This is one of the best places to see these long-tailed parakeets close up. If you walk slowly and quietly along the main tracks you may see one up ahead feeding on the ground before it flies away.

Following the successful eradication of introduced rats and mice in 1988–89, extensive ecological restoration work, including native species plantings, has been successfully carried out by Taranaki Whānui ki Te Upoko o Te Ika, Forest & Bird's Lower Hutt branch, Matiu Somes Island Charitable Trust and the local community. The result is a big increase in numbers of red-crowned kākāriki, pīwakawaka New Zealand fantail and kōtare sacred kingfisher. The other resident native birds here are tūī and riroriro grey warblers, plus there were reports of koekoeā long-tailed cuckoos on the island in February–March 2018.

After you walk up the main road towards the DOC buildings there is a right-hand turn onto the main circuit track around the island, which has spectacular panoramic views. Kekeno New Zealand fur seals sometimes haul out on Shag Rock off the south-west end of the island, which can be viewed from a lookout near the main track. Check carefully if you see a seal because three ihupuku southern elephant seals reportedly came ashore on the island in November 1963.

From 2012 to 2014 over 200 pakahā were translocated to artificial burrows on the island by the Matiu Somes Island

THE HUTT VALLEY

The kōkōwai spotted skink is quite large with small pale spots.

Charitable Trust and the Kaitiaki Board with support from DOC, and birds are now breeding successfully here. Since 2019, pairs of kuaka common diving petrels have also fledged six chicks here, one of which returned and paired up in 2023. These small black-and-white seabirds with blue feet, dubbed 'flying penguins', fly on fast-whirring wings like a big bumble bee and can fly through high waves, going in one side and out the other without hesitation!

Matiu Somes Island is an important breeding site for kawau tikitiki spotted shags and kororā. The kawau tikitiki colonies here are the largest in the region. The birds nest along the steep western side of the island, and on Shag Rock and adjacent Mokopuna Island. The kororā population has grown to 400 pairs since 170 artificial nest boxes were installed. Watch around the wharf and nearby tracks late in the day where you might see one in the water or coming ashore.

Since 1998, taonga reptile species such as tuatara, moko pāpā Raukawa gecko, ngahere gecko, moko kākāriki barking gecko, kōkōwai spotted skink and ornate skink have been successfully released on the island. The skinks like to bask in the sun along the edges of the tracks and the paths by the buildings. Since geckos and tuatara are nocturnal, the best strategy is to look for them at night using a torch with a red light. Tuatara are mostly seen along the main eastern track, while geckos like the visitor centre building and nearby paths. Tuatara are thought to have lived in Aotearoa for 80 million years, and the endemic geckos and skinks probably dispersed here over the past 50 million years.

Since 1996, Cook Strait giant wētā and Wellington tree wētā have also been successfully released on Matiu. The best place to look for giant wētā is at night in the grassy area around the visitor centre building. Abundant flowering koromiko hebe in summer means there is a good chance of seeing butterflies such as kahukōwhai yellow admiral, kahukura red admiral, and pepe para riki North Island coastal copper and Māui's copper. Other interesting insect life to watch out for here includes the New Zealand giant stick insect, kihikihi wawā clapping cicada and whē New Zealand mantis.

GETTING THERE

Ferries to Matiu depart regularly from Queens Wharf and from Ōtuamotoro Days Bay Wharf. You can either return the same day, or overnight in a Forest & Bird house with three bedrooms that is bookable online for a fee. Private boats or kayaks are permitted to land only at the island's main wharf or the beach next to it. The island is open to the public daily between 8.30am and 5pm.

Female New Zealand whē mantis eating male whē.

The striking moko kākāriki barking gecko is named for its vocalisations.

THE HUTT VALLEY

View of beech forest with northern rātā flowering, Ōtuamotoro Days Bay.

20 EAST HARBOUR REGIONAL PARK NORTHERN FOREST

including Ōtuamotoro, Muritai and Butterfly Creek

East Harbour Regional Park is one of the most species-rich wild places in Te Upoko-o-te-Ika. The wetter valleys in the northern forest section have lush podocarp forest with areas of regenerating pukatea and mānuka. On higher terrain, there is tawhai beech forest with areas of northern rātā and kāmahi. Another sublime attraction is the treasure trove of native orchids.

The northern forest section of East Harbour Regional Park (EHRP) has one of the richest orchid floras in the harbour area, with a quarter of the country's 120 native orchid species. Their flowering here is one of the botanical glories of wild Wellington, and will leave you enchanted by their delicate elegance and beautiful fragrances.

The two main ground orchid groups are the sun orchids and the onion orchids, which grow up to 80 centimetres tall. Sun orchid flowers are up to 3 centimetres wide and can form impressive sprays of up to 20 blooms on each plant that mesmerise as they sway around in a light breeze. Onion orchids are pale green with up to a hundred smaller, more densely packed flowers on each plant.

Most of the other species are forest orchids. Among these, hūperei black orchids grow a dark flowering spike up to a metre tall with up to 40 dark greenish-brown and cream-coloured lantern-shaped flowers. The creamy white flowering perching peka-a-waka bamboo orchids and delicate pink-and-white flowering winikā orchid can grow quite large on tree trunks and branches, spreading out for several metres. The flowers of winikā grow up to 3 centimetres wide and form extensive sprays on masses of fine bamboo-like stems. Winikā was formerly also known by the English name Christmas orchid.

The flowers of the sun orchids and *Caladenia* orchids have a striking range of colours, from flamingo pinks and violet mauves to hot pinks and vivid purples. The bamboo orchids and sun orchids are the most fragrant, while the greenhood orchids and *Corybas* spider orchids are the most diverse.

Greenhood orchids can grow up to 50 centimetres tall and have a 'snapdragon' ability to trap insects in their flowers, helping to boost pollination. Their convex hood-shaped flowers are green with opaque white stripes, and

Winikā orchid flower.

have a touch-sensitive 'tongue' that forms a narrow platform at the centre of the flower. When an insect touches the tongue, it snaps back and traps the insect inside the flower. The only way for the insect to escape is to crawl through a small tunnel past the pollen. The tongue then resets itself in about 30 minutes. If you carefully insert a small twig and gently touch the tongue, you can see it snap back.

Many of our native orchid species can self-pollinate. Charles Darwin was baffled by this, eventually conceding that it was a temporary fall-back strategy for when cross-pollination failed during adverse weather conditions.

Most orchids have a complex relationship with soil fungi. For example, the tiny seeds of sun orchids and tutukiwi lack nutrients and have evolved an association with mycorrhizal fungi that provides nutrients to the orchid, which is critical in the early stages of growth. This association can be species-specific for the entire life of the plant.

All of the native forest bird species that have survived naturally in the southern part of Te Ika-a-Māui North Island live here: tūī, korimako bellbird, tītitipounamu rifleman, kōtare sacred kingfisher, kererū New Zealand pigeon, ruru morepork, pōpokotea whitehead, pīwakawaka New Zealand fantail, riroriro grey warbler, pīpīwharauroa shining cuckoo, koekoeā long-tailed cuckoo and kārearea New Zealand falcon.

A trio of reptiles also survive here – mokomoko northern grass skink, copper skink and moko pāpā Raukawa gecko – and the streams are healthy enough to support giant kōkopu, ōrea long-finned eel, tuna short-finned eel, toitoi common bully and banded kōkopu, as well as kōura freshwater crayfish.

The rare endemic pepe pōuri forest ringlet butterfly was last reported in Butterfly Creek in 2016 and at the top of the Kōwhai Track in 2018. Keep an eye out for these orange, brown and cream-coloured beauties in summer, and if you see one, please take photos and report your sighting to *iNaturalist NZ*. A study of the local population recorded a dramatic decline in their caterpillars between 2001 and 2016, probably due to the predations of invasive introduced wasps.

Insects have been described as creating the biological foundation for all terrestrial ecosystems, and there is certainly a wealth of them here, including winged insects such as kahukura red admiral and kahukōwhai yellow admiral butterflies, kapokapowai dragonflies, damselflies and kihikihi cicadas. Among the forest and ground insect marvels here are pāpapa tiger beetles, stick insects, pepeke nguturoa giraffe weevils and various wētā. The amber-brown carnivorous land snail *Wainuia urnula* is also found here.

The native plants in the forest here are a feast for all the senses: the colourful and fragrant orchids, the feathery textures of fern fronds and the peppery taste of kawakawa leaves. The northern forest is also renowned for its native ferns, with about 40 species from giant tree ferns and large ground ferns to the smaller filmy ferns and fork ferns. More than 250 native plant species flourish here in this steep hill country, including the local endemic Edgar's mīkoikoi iris and the regionally

Pepe pōuri forest ringlet butterfly adults live for 3–4 weeks in December–January.

uncommon dark-flowering shrub *Pittosporum divaricatum*.

More than a hundred species of fungi also grow in the park, including coral fungus, bioluminescent mushrooms, the blue werewere-kōkako mushroom *Entoloma hochstetteri*, green verdigris waxcaps and red puapua-a-autahi anemone stinkhorn fungus.

The wealth of biodiversity here highlights why it is important to actively protect our wild places. The park is managed by Greater Wellington Regional Council and volunteer group Mainland Island Restoration Operation (MIRO), which has been maintaining a pest-trapping network in the 2200-hectare northern forest section of the park since 2005 to help protect and restore native habitats and species. MIRO also manage urban pest-trapping in all the Muritai Eastbourne bays to protect the local nesting pohowera banded dotterels, and in Ōtuamotoro Days Bay where kororā little blue penguins nest, and they also have a permit to band and protect the pohowera that nest on the Muritai Eastbourne foreshore.

A series of tracks along the Ōtuamotoro and Muritai coastline become steeper as they rise to the ridge at over 300 metres above sea level. The following three sections describe the three main loop walks, two of which link up with Butterfly Creek. These can be accessed via the number 81, 83 and 84 buses, or in combination with the harbour ferry that connects the city to Ōtuamotoro. There is also limited parking near the start of these tracks.

Ōtuamotoro Days Bay Korimako Track and Kererū Track loop walk

The start of the Kererū Track is a short walk from Ōtuamotoro Days Bay wharf. It then rises along a fern-lined avenue of lowland forest from the south end of the pond in Williams Park. After about 100 metres, take the left-hand turn where a side track takes you about 150 metres to a stile. Turn right at the stile onto Korimako Street, walk about 200 metres to the road end and go through the signposted metal entrance gate where the Korimako Track begins.

From here it winds up another 500 metres through regenerating scrub to a block of tall pine trees with tawhai beech forest on either side. The track continues through here before winding more steeply through regenerating scrub for another 250 metres until reaching mature tawhai forest. The track rises through here to the ridge. Turn right at the ridge, and after about 500 metres turn right down the Kererū Track, which drops very steeply for about a kilometre back to Williams Park. The Kererū Track is very slippery when wet.

This loop is about 4 kilometres and takes about two hours to walk, depending on the pace you set. The ridge section through mature tawhai forest is the best area to listen and watch for pōpokotea whiteheads, pīpīwharauroa shining cuckoos and koekoeā long-tailed cuckoos in spring and summer. I've also heard kākāriki here.

Going up through the tawhai beech forest, also listen and look out for the tītitipounamu rifleman, miromiro North Island tomtit, korimako bellbird, tūī and pīwakawaka New Zealand fantail. Tītitipounamu often forage for insects in small family groups. Te Papa vertebrates curator Colin Miskelly has recently published on how they also eat tawhai beech seeds. Watch for them flicking their wings and foraging by climbing up tree trunks or hanging upside down from branches.

Listen also for the descending song of the riroriro and you might see this subtle silver-grey songbird with a hummingbird-like habit of hovering as it forages for insects. If you do, note how it fans its white-tipped tail when it hovers. Check any dead branches up ahead for kārearea, and for kāhu swamp harrier gliding over the ridge.

The butterflies here in summer are kahukōwhai yellow admirals and kahukura red admirals. Pāpapa tiger beetles, Wellington tree wētā and pēpeke nguturoa giraffe weevils are sometimes seen on or near the track.

The northern rātā above Ōtuamotoro

Female tītitipounamu rifleman, our smallest bird species.

Riroriro grey warbler is our most widely distributed endemic bird species.

Northern rātā flower.

Northern rātā flowering.

Māikaika spotted sun orchid, flamingo pink.

Māikaika spotted sun orchid, mauve.

Grasshopper on māikaika spotted sun orchid.

Māikaika spotted sun orchid, blue spots.

Days Bay is the largest stand of intact terrestrial rātā forest in the region. Viewable to the north from the Korimako Track shortly after the pine block, it is spectacular in its summer crimson blush. Rewarewa, kāmahi and hīnau also flower near the track in October–January, and look out for the attractive (but poisonous) tūrutu New Zealand blueberry, which flowers in November–December before producing its blue-purple berries in December–May.

This loop track is a native orchid 'hot spot', with the best time for flowering usually November–February. There are probably more native orchid species here (25) than at any of the other park tracks, making it the most accessible place with the widest range of native orchids in the harbour area.

Sun orchids are so-called because they need sunshine, warmth, and relatively still conditions for their flowers to open fully, which usually occurs between midday and mid-afternoon. They grow on open areas of clay banks or soils. Māikaika spotted sun orchids flower in November–December next to both these tracks, but mostly by the Korimako, between the metal entrance gate and the start of the upper tawhai forest. Their flower colours are highly variable, ranging from pale lavender to vivid purple, pastel pink to hot pink, or deep magenta to white with deep blue spots.

The other sun orchid species that flower here in November–December are maikuku common sun orchid (lower track to upper tawhai forest), Hatch's sun orchid (pine block to upper tawhai forest) and slender sun orchid (lower track before pine block), which range from white to roseate to pale blue, as well as the delicate 'purple fingers' form of the common sun orchid (just before the metal stile). All this makes the Korimako Track a floral 'lucky dip' in early summer.

From mid-October to early December the white and pink flowering *Caladenia chlorostyla* 'red stem' and 'green fingers' varieties flower from the lower track to the upper tawhai forest, and both the pink-flowering *C. variegata* and pink-white flowering *C. bartlettii* flower from the lower track before the pine block to the upper tawhai forest. Their beautiful flowers have quite variable finger-like petals and sepals that are suggestive of bowing ballet dancers with arms held out gracefully at each side.

The tall hūperei black orchids produce their greenish-brown and cream-coloured, lantern-like flowers in November–January (upper tawhai forest), the spurred helmet orchid flowers in May–July (just after the metal entrance gate), and the dark magenta flowering spider orchid *Corybas trilobus* 'remutaka' flowers in August–December (pine block and upper tawhai forest).

More than 20 *Corybas* spider orchid species have been recorded in Aotearoa so far. The most variable are those

THE HUTT VALLEY

included under the name *C. trilobus*. Te Papa botany curator Carlos Lehnebach and colleagues have segregated and described five new species from this group, but more may exist; some, such as the abovementioned 'remutaka', currently have only 'tag names' and await investigation. Some spider orchids form dense colonies that carpet the ground along moist banks or next to forest tracks. Their flowers have long thin petals and sepals that look almost like 'arms', giving them a spider-like appearance. Most flower in September–November.

The beautiful larger white-and-pink flowers of the winikā orchid bloom in November–December (upper beech forest), while the creamy-white flowers of the peka-a-waka bamboo orchid appear in October–December on the ground and tree trunks (upper tawhai forest). The raupeka Easter orchid flowers on the ground and fallen tree trunks here during February–April. Its porcelain-white flowers fill the tawhai forest with their heady sweet scent, and to watch a kahukura red admiral butterfly sail over them in a sunlit glade and land to feed on their nectar with the forest towering above is a memorable experience.

Pygmy tree orchid, fleshy green tree orchid and spotted green tree orchid all grow in the upper tawhai forest, but the latter is very rare due to past illegal collection. The green-and-maroon pixie cap orchid flowers in the pine block in June–September, the green maikaika common onion orchid grows by the track (metal entrance gate to pine block) in November–December, and the maroon-and-green horned orchid grows just before the pine block in December–January.

Among the greenhood orchids, *Pterostylis cardiostigma* was first described from a specimen collected in Ōtuamotoro. It and two others (*P. banksii, P. australis*) flower in the pine block in September–December, while winter greenhood orchid flowers here in April–August. The grass-leaved greenhood orchid flowers by the first section of the Korimako Track in October–December, trowel-leaved greenhood orchid in June–August, and New Zealand mountain greenhood orchid *P. montana* in November.

The Kererū Track has comparatively fewer species (nine): maikuku and māikaika spotted sun orchids, peka-a-waka, raupeka, winikā, green fleshy tree orchid, winter greenhood, *Caladenia chlorostyla* and *Corybas trilobus*.

The tall tree ferns that grow along the Kererū Track include mamaku black tree fern, kātote soft tree fern and ponga silver fern. The smaller ground ferns here, such as raurenga kidney fern and kōwaowao hound's tongue fern, are abundant near the stream crossing on the way up the Kererū. Matua mauku filmy fern, fan-like filmy fern and screw fern are more widespread.

If you take the ferry from the city to

Caladenia chlorostyla 'red stem'.

Caladenia chlorostyla 'green fingers'.

Caladenia variegata orchid.

Maikuku common sun orchid.

Hatch's sun orchid, pink.

Hūperei black orchid flower.

Raupeka Easter orchid.

Silver-back spider orchid *Corybas macranthus*.

Spider orchid *Corybas trilobus* 'remutaka'.

Trowel-leaved greenhood orchids.

Horned orchid.

Mamaku black tree fern, our largest tree fern species, in tawhai beech forest.

Raurenga kidney fern.

Patch of winter greenhood orchids.

THE HUTT VALLEY

Maikaika common onion orchid.

Mackenzie Track and Muritai Track

These two tracks start at about sea level in Muritai Eastbourne and converge near the top of the ridge, so can be walked from either end. The Mackenzie is the more gradual of the two, with more open sections. Both pass through sections of tawhai beech forest. At the point where they both converge there is an option to walk over the saddle and down into the upper section of Butterfly Creek.

The Mackenzie Track is signposted off Muritai Road opposite Karamu Street, starting on the left 50 metres along MacKenzie Road. This track has three wooden benches, the third of which is located near the junction with the Muritai Track. It takes about an hour to walk to the top of the track depending on the pace you set.

The Mackenzie Track starts with a set of steps before rising through regenerating forest with māhoe and rangiora, some mānuka scrub and sections of tawhai forest. As you near the top, do not take the left-hand junction with the main ridge track north. A little further past that is the right-hand junction with the Muritai Track. Continue past this to stay on the Mackenzie Track. It takes you over a saddle before dropping down into the north end of Butterfly Creek. It takes about 30 minutes to walk along the creek to a junction with the Kōwhai Track and

Ōtuamotoro Days Bay, keep an eye out for maki orca. Two adults and a calf were seen from the ferry off Muritai Eastbourne and Ōtuamotoro on 8 November 2019, and a pod of five were seen close to Ōtuamotoro wharf before they swam south towards Muritai on 27 October 2022.

GETTING THERE

In addition to the ferry from the city, the 81, 83 and 84 buses all stop in Ōtuamotoro Days Bay. There is parking by Williams Park near the start of both tracks.

another 15 minutes to the picnic area where the track ends. This track can be soggy and muddy in winter. You can either return via the same route and go down the Muritai Track, or via the Kōwhai Track, which is a shorter route of about 30 minutes.

The native birds here are much the same as in Ōtuamotoro, but kārearea New Zealand falcon, pōpokotea whitehead, korimako bellbird and miromiro North Island tomtit are seen less frequently. Mokomoko northern grass skinks are often seen basking in the morning sun by the side of the open sections of the Mackenzie Track in spring and summer. Walk slowly and quietly while looking down for them. Most are pale caramel and brown, but a few can be dark chocolate-brown.

The entrance to the Muritai Track is signposted at the end of an alley running east by 261 Muritai Road. The track zigzags uphill through regenerating forest containing two sections of tawhai forest with hīnau, nīkau, tītoki and rewarewa, and an understorey of mingimingi and hangehange New Zealand privet. It takes about an hour to reach the top where it meets the Mackenzie Track.

This loop walk is also a native orchid 'hot spot'. One notable species that grows by both tracks is the green bird orchid, which flowers in November–December. Check for it in the area where the two tracks meet. Higher up alongside the Mackenzie you may spot *Caladenia* orchids in October–December. Both the 'white fingers' and 'red stem' varieties of *C. chlorostyla* are present here, plus the less common 'minor' variety and the pink-flowering *C. variegata*.

Maikaika common onion orchids flower along the mid-section of the Mackenzie in November–December. Among the greenhood orchids, tutukiwi and grass-leaved greenhood flower in September–December, winter greenhood in April–August, trowel-leaved greenhood in June–August and *Pterostylis cardiostigma* in November–December.

Maikuku common sun orchids and māikaika spotted sun orchids flower in November–December along the middle and upper Mackenzie Track, from where the mānuka scrub ends up to the top. The 'purple fingers' form of the common sun orchid flowers in early December and Hatch's sun orchid in November–December. Both grow by the track just past the mānuka scrub.

Hūperei black orchids flower in December–January by the tawhai forest sections of the Mackenzie, and winikā flowers in December along the upper sections of both tracks. Raupeka Easter orchid is widespread on the upper Mackenzie, where it flowers in February–March, and the pixie cap orchid grows by both tracks, flowering in June–September.

The Muritai Track has fleshy green tree orchid and raupeka orchid growing in the tawhai forest in the upper track area. Pixie cap orchid (flowering June–September), the pinkish maroon gnat orchid (August–October), the spider orchid *Corybas trilobus* (October–November) and maikuku common sun orchid all grow along the first half of the Muritai.

Hūperei black orchid flowers along the lower tawhai forest section of the Muritai in high summer. Slender sun orchid (December), pixie cap orchid, raupeka orchid, and peka-a-waka bamboo orchid also flower along the north section of Butterfly Creek.

The relatively modest variety of ferns by the Mackenzie Track includes ponga silver fern, button fern, puhinui Cunningham's maidenhair fern and kōwaowao hound's tongue fern. The Muritai Track passes some lush gullies and has some damp trackside banks, so the fern diversity is greater, including screw fern, small kiokio, rauranga kidney fern, mouku hen and chickens fern and the ancient-looking fork ferns.

Some other notable native plants that grow by these tracks include tūrutu New Zealand blueberry, Edgar's mīkoikoi iris and rimuroa violet harebell. Pikirangi native red mistletoe, which flowers in November–January, used to be more abundant in the park, and although very few individual plants are now known in the area (on private land), efforts are under way to bring them back.

Among the colourful fungi that sprout along the Mackenzie in autumn and winter are lilac and red *Clavaria* coral fungi, violet potato fungus, blue-green potato fungus and the New Zealand endemic straw flycap, which grows in a mycorrhizal association with tawhai forest. The Muritai has the bioluminescent harore lemon honeycap mushroom *Armillaria limonea*, New Zealand native shiitake mushroom, southern false morel and the eye-catching velvet earthstar – a strange fungus species that grows as a small, spherical ball until its outer skin splits and peels back in a star-like pattern around the spore sac. The sac then develops a pore, through which the earthstar puffs out its 'stardust' of brown spores.

The north end of Butterfly Creek has some charismatic fungi including blue werewere-kōkako *Entoloma hochstetteri*, red puapua-a-autahi anemone stinkhorn fungus and green verdigris waxcap.

Walking along Butterfly Creek can leave you feeling as though you have escaped the bustle of city life into a secluded realm. It has big kahikatea, rimu, nīkau, tawa, rewarewa and lush kiekie, and many ground ferns including waekura umbrella fern, filmy ferns, mokimoki fragrant fern and huruhuru tapairu maidenhair ferns. The tawhai forest here flowers in summer and there are wahu tall sundews and rock harebell (*Wahlenbergia matthewsii*) by the tracks. These pink-flowering sundews lure, trap and digest insects by producing a sticky secretion.

Pixie cap orchid.

Mokimoki fragrant fern.

Puhinui Cunningham's maidenhair fern.

Green verdigris waxcap.

Harore lemon honeycap mushrooms.

Wahu tall sundew flowers.

THE HUTT VALLEY

Pikirangi native red mistletoe flowering.

The native birds here are similar to those at Ōtuamotoro, including tītitipounamu rifleman, and in spring and summer both cuckoos – pīpīwharauroa and koekoeā – are possible. The native freshwater fish species in Butterfly Creek and nearby Gollans Stream include giant kōkopu, banded kōkopu, red-finned bully, īnanga and ōrea long-finned eels.

GETTING THERE

The number 81, 83 and 84 buses stop on Muritai Street near the start of both tracks, going in both directions. There are limited road parking options.

Kōwhai Track and Korohiwa Track circuit connecting with lower Butterfly Creek

The start of the Kōwhai Track is signposted at the end of Kōwhai Street in Eastbourne. It is a shorter and steeper track than the Korohiwa (formerly Bus Barn) Track, which starts further south by Muritai bus terminus.

The track rises in sharp zigzags and offers a spectacular view back across the harbour. After the first bench, it passes mānuka scrub and rises through sections of native forest where pink-flowering wahu tall sundews, fragrant flowering hangehange and various greenhood orchids grow by the track. White-flowering puawānanga native clematis, cream-flowering kaihua native jasmine and white-flowering pōānanga Forster's clematis can usually be seen climbing through the trackside bushes.

After about 500 metres, the Kōwhai Track meets the ridgeline at a three-way junction with the north end of the Korohiwa Track near a wooden bench. It takes about 30 minutes to walk up this far, depending on your pace. The Kōwhai Track drops down from the ridge to meet the south end of Butterfly Creek. At the junction with the creek, you can turn right and walk to the picnic area. A return walk from the start of the Kōwhai to the picnic area takes about two hours.

Alternatively, at the three-way junction at the saddle you can turn right and walk south up and along the ridge section of the Korohiwa Track until it veers downhill to the bus terminus, which takes about one hour in total. Another option is to walk up the Korohiwa from near the bus terminus and back down the Kōwhai, giving Butterfly Creek a miss.

The Korohiwa Track winds uphill through regenerating scrub including hangehange, kāmahi, whauwhaupaku five-finger and hīnau. Higher up there is tawhai forest and porokaiwhiri pigeonwood, māhoe, tītoki and nīkau. Eventually the track reaches the ridge, where there is tall tawhai forest.

Pōānanga Forster's clematis flowering.

There is a similar mix of lowland podocarp and tawhai forest on either side of the Kōwhai as it drops down into Butterfly Creek. The lowland podocarp forest has mature rimu, miro, matai and kahikatea, but the presence of tree ferns, kiekie and perching lilies also gives it a lush, subtropical feel. This tranquil and secluded stream valley ends at an open picnic area just over a small wooden bridge that crosses Gollans Stream.

The birds seen along both tracks are mostly tūī, korimako bellbird, pīwakawaka New Zealand fantail, riroriro grey warbler and tauhou silvereye, with the chance of hearing or seeing kārearea New Zealand

Hūperei black orchid.

Gnat orchid.

Tutukiwi common greenhood orchid.

falcon. Listen and look out for miromiro North Island tomtit in the taller tawhai forest at the top of the Korohiwa, and for kāhu swamp harriers and kārearea from the open sections while going up. Kererū New Zealand pigeons sometimes fly overhead, too.

Once you drop down the Kōwhai into Butterfly Creek there is the chance of hearing or seeing kākāriki and pīpīwharauroa shining cuckoos in summer, and tītitipounamu rifleman can forage close to the track.

The native orchids alongside the higher sections of the Kōwhai on this side include tutukiwi common greenhood, maikuku common sun, māikaika spotted

Kihitara red damselfly.

sun, raupeka Easter and hūperei black. Tutukiwi grow quite tall – up to 25 centimetres – near the saddle. Hūperei grows near the saddle and the start of the Kōwhai. This orchid grows underground in potato-like tubers for most of the year, where it stores carbohydrates and nutrients gleaned from *Armillaria* and other fungi, which in turn are mainly parasitic on woody plants. This relationship, in which a plant parasitises a fungus to obtain nutrients rather than by photosynthesis, is known as myco-heterotrophy. Hūperei grow a single tall, dark stalk which produces a series of dark green and creamy-white lantern-like flowers in December–January.

Where the Kōwhai drops down into Butterfly Creek is a good section to look for the spider orchid *Corybas trilobus*, silver-back spider orchid *C. macranthus* and the big red spider orchid *C. iridescens*, all of which flower in September–October. Raupeka also flowers here in February–March.

Maikuku, māikaika, grass-leaved greenhood orchid and hūperei flower in December–January alongside the south end of Butterfly Creek, and pygmy tree orchid produces its distinctive tiny bulbs in November.

Maikuku, pixie cap orchid and gnat orchid grow by the lower to middle Korohiwa. Winter greenhood orchid, tutukiwi, *Pterostylis cardiostigma*, *P. australis*, *Corybas trilobus* and *C. macranthus* also grow alongside the upper section of the Korohiwa, including the ridge section. Both of the green tree orchid species grow in the tawhai forest along the ridge, flowering in November–December, the spotted species only in very small numbers due to past illegal collection.

A wooden bench next to the tawhai forest where the Korohiwa reaches the south end of the ridge has a good view. Watch for kererū, tītitipounamu, riroriro and kahukura red admiral butterflies here, and pixie cap orchid sometimes grows nearby.

Butterfly Creek has an interesting diversity of dragonflies in summer including the kapokapowai New Zealand bush giant dragonfly, ranger dragonfly, blue-spotted hawker and the scarce dusk dragonfly. Both blue and red damselflies are often seen by the small wooden bridge crossing Gollans Steam to the picnic area. Other interesting insects include the New Zealand striped longhorn beetle, elephant weevil, steel-blue ladybird and pāpapa tiger beetle.

The ferns are equally diverse, ranging from the large mamaku and ponga to the smaller ring fern, raurenga kidney fern, fan-like filmy fern and irirangi drooping filmy fern. Umbrella moss also grows near the top of the Korohiwa.

Among the many fungi that pepper the upper track are pink gill, blackening waxcap, the bioluminescent harore lemon honeycap mushroom *Armillaria limonea*, southern beech amanita and the rare southern false morel. Even more colourful are lilac coral fungus, violet potato fungus and red puapua-a-autahi anemone stinkhorn fungus.

From Kōwhai Street it is only a short walk to the foreshore via a public alleyway next to 374 Muritai Road. Pohowera banded dotterels nest on the stony foreshore on the coast inside a large, fenced-off area in summer. Watch for these small shorebirds standing on top of big stones, but be careful not to get too close to them or their nests or chicks. The beach here is a good place to look for giant horse mussel and common fan scallop shells among the sea sponges and seaweeds that wash ashore after storms.

GETTING THERE

The number 81, 83 and 84 buses all stop on Muritai Street near house number 383 (southbound) and house number 378 (northbound) near the start of the Kōwhai Track, and all terminate at the Bus Barn terminal at 493 Muritai Street. The start of the Korohiwa Track is immediately next to the terminus on the south side. There is limited parking near the start of both tracks.

Kiekie.

Pāpapa tiger beetle.

Kēkēwai blue damselfly.

Lake Kōhangapiripiri: small arm.

21 PARANGARAHU LAKES AT TE RAE-AKIAKI

The Parangarahu Lakes – Kōhangaterā and Kōhangapiripiri – sit within the southern section of East Harbour Regional Park behind Te Rae-akiaki Pencarrow Head by the south-east coast. These tranquil taonga lakes with their unique community of native species are described by the Department of Conservation as the last remaining, relatively unmodified wetlands in the region.

Public access to the Parangarahu Lakes – Kōhangatera and Kōhangapiripiri – is via a coastal gravel track that begins at Burdan's Gate at the southern end of Eastbourne. They cannot be reached from the Butterfly Creek picnic area even though it joins with Gollans Stream and flows down to Lake Kōhangatera, because there is no streamside track.

These lakes are habitat for a healthy diversity of freshwater fishes, including tuna short-finned eel and ōrea long-finned eel, giant kōkopu, banded kōkopu, toitoi common bully and tītarakura giant bully. There are also kōura freshwater crayfish, kākahi freshwater mussels and freshwater snails here.

Adult weweia New Zealand dabchick on the water.

The main wetland plants are raupō and kuta lake clubrush, with toetoe and swamp buttercup nearby. About 30 bird species have been recorded in the vicinity including kakīānau black swan, pūkeko, pārera grey duck and kuruwhengi Australasian shoveler. Pāpango New Zealand scaup are present in the warmer months, pūtangitangi paradise shelducks in autumn, and a few tētē grey teal visit both lakes. Above the ducks, warou welcome swallows fly around hawking for their small insect prey.

The weweia New Zealand dabchick breeds year-round at the 11-hectare Lake Kōhangapiripiri and is present on the 17-hectare Lake Kōhangatera. This small endemic grebe with rufous neck feathers and bright yellow eyes dives down in the lake to catch small freshwater fish, kōura and kākahi with its dagger-like bill.

The more elusive pūweto spotless crake lives in the raupō past the north end of Lake Kōhangapiripiri through to the boardwalk and the large raupō bed at the south-east end of Lake Kōhangatera. This small, dark bluish-grey and brown rail, with stout black bill, pinkish legs and red eyes, is more often heard than seen. Listen for its bubbling and trilling 'lawnmower' calls.

Three kawau shag species (black, little black, little pied) sometimes feed on fish or eels in the lakes; the largest of these is the imposing māpunga black shag, which can grow up to 88 centimetres and weigh up to 2.4 kilograms. This serpentine bird is black with white-feathered cheeks and throat, yellow facial skin, green eyes and a long grey bill with a hooked tip. Māpunga will also eat young ducklings.

Another apex predator recorded here is the cryptic matuku-hūrepo Australasian bittern. This is the 'tiger heron' of the raupō, stealthily ambushing unsuspecting eel and fish prey, stabbing at them with its heavy, yellowish spear bill. Its tawny plumage has tiger-like caramel and chocolate-coloured stripes and streaks. Unfortunately, it is also one of our most threatened bird species, listed as critically endangered along with the kākāpō. Like kākāpō, male bitterns make a series of *wooom-wooom* booming calls during the breeding season.

From August to January, pohowera banded dotterels nest in the tundra-like habitat on the stony raised beach between sparse mat daisies, pinātoro New Zealand daphne and horokaka New Zealand ice-plant. These endearing small brown-and-white plovers have big dark eyes, a short black bill and long dark legs. In breeding plumage, the male can be distinguished by a chestnut breast band with a second narrower black neck band above it. The female also has these bands but they are quite dull.

Pest trapping, local rāhui and new signage in the area are all helping to increase the breeding success of the

Kōtare sacred kingfisher.

pohowera here. The local coastal plant community also includes pīngao, kōwhangatara spinifex, panahi shore bindweed and sand buttercup. It is important to respect the nesting birds and their delicate cushion plant habitat by avoiding trampling on any nests or plants.

Pīhoihoi New Zealand pipits and tōrea pango variable oystercatchers also breed along the raised stony beaches here, with tōrea South Island pied oystercatchers and poaka pied stilts sometimes visiting in summer. White-faced herons also visit this area.

The yellow-banded kapokapowai New Zealand bush giant dragonfly patrols the swampy landscape at the north end of Lake Kōhangatera, hawking for kihikihi cicadas and pēpepe butterflies. They are in turn preyed on by the local kōtare sacred kingfishers. The swamp habitat is also suitable for the ranger dragonfly, Gray's dragonfly and blue-spotted hawker.

Māpunga black shag is an apex predator at the lakes.

Matuku-hūrepo Australasian bittern is the 'tiger heron' of the raupō.

Pohowera banded dotterel female in habitat.　　Horokaka New Zealand ice plant.

Mat daisy and pinātoro New Zealand daphne, nesting habitat of pohowera banded dotterel.

Since 2013, Greater Wellington Regional Council (GWRC) and volunteer group Mainland Island Restoration Organisation (MIRO) have been working to protect and restore pohowera in the Parangarahu Lakes Area, including pest trapping and bird banding. Monitoring by MIRO commenced in 2016. Since 2022, monitoring and pest trapping has been done in partnership with the Hem of Remutaka, a project led by Taranaki Whānui ki Te Upoko o Te Ika in partnership with Conservation Volunteers New Zealand, Department of Conservation, and GWRC with Friends of Baring Head and MIRO, Orongorongo Station and Pencarrow Station.

MIRO commenced planting native species here in 2007. Rōpū Tiaki, the guardianship and co-governance group of Taranaki Whānui and GWRC for the Parangarahu Lakes Area, has also been planting native species and using local rāhui and new signage to help protect pohowera breeding sites since 2012. It also helped restore aquatic life at Zealandia Te Māra a Tāne with the translocation of kākahi freshwater mussels and toitoi common bully from Lake Kōhangapiripiri to Roto Māhanga in 2022 and 2023.

GETTING THERE/AROUND

The number 81, 83 and 84 buses run regularly from Wellington bus station and Queensgate bus terminus in Hutt City to the Muritai 'Bus Barn' bus terminus. From here it is possible to walk about 300 metres south to the Wildfinder depot at 519 Muritai Road, which has mountain bikes, e-bikes and children's bikes for hire. From here you can cycle south from Burdan's Gate along the coastal gravel road to the lakes. It is 7 kilometres to the Lake Kōhangapiripiri outlet into Fitzroy Bay, then about another kilometre to the Lake Kōhangatera outlet into Fitzroy Bay.

The track that starts on the western side of Lake Kōhangapiripiri goes up to the lighthouse, which offers views east across the lake, and another track that runs part way along the eastern side of the lake. There is also a track that runs along the eastern side of Lake Kōhangatera. It is advisable to choose a day without strong winds.

There is limited parking at the southern end of Muritai Street near the locked gate. The walk from the gate out to the lakes is long but flat. There are occasional guided bus tours that drive all the way out to the lakes; these are run by GWRC and advertised on its website. Treated sewage and effluent is discharged into the sea via a pipe at Te Rae-akiaki Pencarrow Head, so swimming and gathering kaimoana are not recommended in this area.

Panorama view from the Puketahā maunga.

22 PUKETAHĀ FOREST IN WAINUIOMATA MAINLAND ISLAN

This spectacular ancient podocarp forest below Puketahā maunga has been described as the most intact in the southern part of the motu, with a staggering 18,000 mature rimu trees covering about 80 percent of the valley. The great swathe of old-growth podocarps dominates the forest canopy of northern rātā, hīnau, rewarewa and tawa.

Above the podocarp forest there is also 'goblin forest', comprising gnarled tawhai beech trees covered in thick green pūkohu mosses and angiangi lichens, and there is a sweeping view from the maunga itself, 767 metres above sea level. These *Nothofagus* beech forests of Aotearoa are thought by some authorities to be relicts of the ancient forests of Gondwana.

The final refuge of the extinct huia was to the north in the Tararua Range, where it was last recorded in 1907. The last official sighting of kākāpō in the wild in Te Ika-a-Māui North Island was on the northern boundary of adjacent Whitemans Valley in 1905. The extinct mātuhituhi bush wren was recorded in the nearby Remutaka Range in the nineteenth century, but there have been no sightings anywhere in Te Ika-a-Māui since 1955.

The native forest here was spared from logging when it was set aside as a water catchment area in the nineteenth century and now has the healthiest regional populations of most of the naturally surviving common native bird species, especially tītitipounamu rifleman and miromiro New Zealand tomtit. There are also about 20 pairs of kiwi-nui North Island brown kiwi in the area, originating from a 2006 reintroduction to nearby Remutaka Regional Park by the Remutaka Conservation Trust, which has been monitoring the increasing kiwi population and trapping pests there ever since.

Rimu giant.

The Puketahā forest sits within the Wainuiomata Mainland Island established by Greater Wellington Regional Council (GWRC) in 2005, which is itself within the Wainuiomata water catchment area north-east of Wainuiomata Regional Park. At the moment, the only way to visit is to join one of the ranger-guided summer walks notified on the GWRC website as 'Wainuiomata Old Forest Walk'. These start at the main gate along

The view through the foliage of this 1300-year-old mataī giant is like a stained-glass window in a great cathedral.

Whitcher Grove in Wainuiomata and involve walking a 10-kilometre return route through tall native forest and across several stream tributaries of the Wainuiomata River.

During this walk, you will see just how impressively tall the rimu, mataī, kahikatea and northern rātā are – but expect to get a few sore neck muscles! You will also see how each of the older trees looks like an ecosystem in itself, dripping with perching lilies, native orchids, ferns, pūkohu mosses and angiangi lichens. Angiangi are very slow-growing, with some species thought to live for hundreds or even thousands of years.

Native orchids that grow here include perching winikā orchids and peka-a-waka bamboo orchids, as well as raupeka Easter, greenhood and hūperei black orchids. There are also the varied colours and forms of scarlet rātā vine, orange-fruiting porokaiwhiri pigeonwood and yellow-orange fruiting swamp lawyer. Another forest giant here is reputedly the world's tallest moss species, the giant moss *Dawsonia superba*, which grows up to 60 centimetres high. The te reo Māori name, pāhau-kākāpō, means 'moustache of the kākāpō', likening it to the bird's facial whiskers.

There is also an abundance of tree ferns, including luxurious whekī rough tree fern, kātote soft-tree fern and pūnui slender tree fern, and lustrous filmy ferns such as fan-like filmy fern and raurenga

Lichen-covered tree trunk.

Piupiu crown fern.

kidney fern. The greatest diversity is among the ground ferns, with such emerald gems as kiokio palm-leaf fern, rereti lance fern and kiwakiwa water fern.

Higher up the maunga, there are piupiu crown ferns in the goblin forest, and some interesting montane species including the deliciously fragrant creamy-white flowering mountain toropapa and the white-flowering kama bush snowberry. The elevation here is high enough for snow to settle in winter.

In summer, good numbers of kererū New Zealand pigeons and tūī soar and

Small kiokio palm-leaf fern.

Moko kākāriki barking gecko.

Perching winikā orchids.

There are about 20 pairs of kiwi-nui North Island brown kiwi in the area.

Inside the tawhai beech goblin forest.

dive over the podocarp forest, korimako bellbirds and pīpīwharauroa shining cuckoos dart through the canopy, and miromiro North Island tomtits and tītitipounamu riflemen forage in the understorey. All are wary of their aerial nemesis, the kārearea New Zealand falcon. Check any kārearea you see just in case it is the very similar-looking koekoeā long-tailed cuckoo. Listen out for the koekoeā's loud, rising *zzhweeeesht* calls, which often end with a rapid, insistent *pe-pe-pe-pe-pe-pe-pe*, and for the chattering of yellow-crowned kākāriki.

As you turn off the sealed road into the forest you step into the realm of Tāne – in te ao Māori, te rangatiratanga o Tāne. This is where you encounter some of the largest taonga mataī trees, which are about 1300 years old. Looking up at the light radiating through the lush foliage and perching lilies I was reminded of the stained-glass windows of a great cathedral.

Colourful kahukura red admiral and kahukōwhai yellow admiral butterflies flit around in summer, but the graceful pepe pōuri forest ringlet butterfly has not been reported in the valley since 2013, probably due to the predations of invasive introduced wasps on its caterpillars.

The variety of moths here includes the imaginatively named green carpet owlet moth and brown forest flash; among other insect life, check for the pepeke nguturoa giraffe weevil, ground wētā and kapokapowai New Zealand bush giant dragonfly.

GWRC keeps invasive introduced species at low levels here using a network of traps, bait stations and hunting. Doing so has enabled native species to thrive and kiwi-nui to make their own way here from the adjacent Remutaka Forest Park.

There is now an ambitious proposal,

The kākāpō is the only flightless parrot species and one of the longest-lived bird species.

supported by Taranaki Whānui ki Te Upoko o Te Ika, the Department of Conservation (DOC) and GWRC, to establish a predator-free Puketahā ecosanctuary here. The aim is to install a 28-kilometre predator-proof fence around 3300 hectares of the Wainuiomata Water Catchment, then eradicate the invasive pest animals inside the fence before reintroducing kākāpō and other endangered species, including hihi stitchbird and rowi Ōkarito brown kiwi or kiwi pukupuku little spotted kiwi. The ecosanctuary, if established, would be some 15 times larger than the Zealandia ecosanctuary.

The critically endangered moss-green kākāpō is one of the most remarkable birds in the world. It is a nocturnal forest giant, with males reaching 64 centimetres long and weighing up to 4 kilograms. It is the only flightless parrot species and one of the longest-lived bird species, with a reported lifespan of up to 100 years. Like kea, kākāpō can tolerate snow. The late kākāpō researcher Don Merton once described to me how he saw kākāpō living in tunnels underneath snow in Fiordland for months during the winter of 1974.

A detailed feasibility study published in 2021 identified the other threatened or at-risk species that would benefit from reintroduction here as including kōkako, tīeke saddleback, kākā, hihi, red-crowned kākāriki and Cook Strait giant wētā. It estimated the ecosanctuary could provide breeding habitat for up to 150 kākāpō, 2000 pairs of hihi and 500–700 pairs of kōkako.

The surviving reptiles in the area would also benefit, including the mokopirirakau form of ngahere gecko, moko kākāriki barking gecko and moko pāpā Raukawa gecko. The good water quality here is reflected in the healthy diversity of freshwater fish in the streams and awa, which include many of the *Galaxias* fishes (giant kōkopu, kōaro, dwarf galaxias, short-jawed kōkopu) plus toitoi common bully, piharau lamprey and both tuna short-finned and ōrea long-finned eels. The carnivorous land snail *Wainuia urnula* is also found here.

GETTING THERE

The number 160 and 170 buses stop on Main Road in Wainuiomata near the junction with Gibbs Crescent, close to Moores Valley Road. The entrance to the water catchment area is the first right turn 2 kilometres along Moores Valley Road into Whitcher Grove, which turns into Reservoir Road. There is parking near the gate.

Bush walk, Percy Scenic Reserve.

23 PERCY SCENIC RESERVE AND ALPINE PLANT COLLECTION

This compact 14-hectare reserve on the edge of Pito One Petone with origins dating back more than a century has an outstanding variety of native plants, including the most comprehensive collection of native alpine plants in Aotearoa. The diverse native plants growing in the reserve attract some of our best-known native forest songsters.

In spring, the melodic chimes and whistles of korimako bellbird and tūī ring out here as fresh as the first golden flush of the kōwhai. Tūī are especially pleasing to watch in flight with their boisterous energy, repeatedly flying high before diving steeply, as if supercharged with nectar.

Kererū New Zealand pigeons and pōpokatea whiteheads also come in to feed in the trees here. If you see a kererū on a branch, watch how its iridescent purple-bronze and green plumage shimmers in the sun. Listen out for the buzzing calls and melodic song of pōpokatea in the bush, where these highly mobile, sparrow-sized birds spend most of their time gleaning insects in extended family groups.

Pūtangitangi paradise shelducks sometimes visit the pond here from nearby Te Awa Kairangi Hutt River. Both the male and female are feathered heavyweights, but can be distinguished by their plumage. The adult female is a rich chestnut with a white head and upper neck, while the more sombre adult male is charcoal overall with a black head. Both have a chestnut undertail and black-and-green wing feathers with white on the upper surface. The male makes a goose-like honk in flight, or when alarmed; the female makes a rather shrill, rapid and persistent honk, mainly in flight.

A garden was planted on this site by the three Percy brothers in the nineteenth century, with a preference for native species over introduced. That passed into public ownership in 1949, after which the reserve was opened to the public.

The reserve has 2 kilometres of track to explore, as well as a small waterfall and stream. The higher northern part of the reserve has māhoe–tawa forest with kohekohe, mamaku black tree fern and kiekie. Lower down, there is regenerating ngaio, rangiora and māpou. The lower part also has a threatened species garden including Waitākere rock koromiko, Manawatāwhi Three Kings kaikōmako and Gardner's tree daisy.

On the left side of the lower entrance area is a fenced alpine rock garden and a series of glasshouses and shade houses where hundreds of native plant species are grown, including alpine plants, in a climate-controlled environment. Although this area is not routinely open to the public, there are occasional open days when reserve staff run guided tours, and group tours can be requested via Hutt City Council. October is a good month for alpine plant flowering.

Other notable native plants in the reserve include heketara tree daisy, perching kohukohu, karaka and nīkau, as well as seven cultivated specimens of rātā moehau Bartlett's rātā, one of which flowers in summer. Near the lower entrance and opposite the threatened species garden you can see akakaiore native passionfruit, kōnini creeping fuchsia and mākaka native brooms

THE HUTT VALLEY

The pūtangitangi paradise shelduck (male) is a striking goose-like endemic duck.

The adult female pūtangitangi has a white head.

flowering in summer, and there are native ferns including kōwaowao hound's tongue fern, puhinui Cunningham's maidenhair fern and karuwhai climbing shield fern.

The reserve's unique collection of more than a thousand native plant species and varieties is mostly held in the glasshouses, with a selection grown in the alpine rock garden. Many of these were gifted by local botanists Tony and Helen Druce. There are also rare and threatened plants from around Te Upoko-o-te-Ika and threatened ecosystems across Aotearoa, including a fern collection, a forget-me-not collection and a neinei *Dracophyllum* collection.

The reserve is administered by Hutt City Council, with management of the collection carried out as part of the council's contract with Downer Group New Zealand to manage local parks and reserves.

In addition to maintaining the plants here, collection curators Cliff Keilty and John van den Hoeven organise expeditions to alpine areas to collect seeds and plant cuttings for propagation in the nursery area to add to the collection. In recent years they have organised expeditions to Ōpuke Mt Hutt, Kawarau Gorge, The Remarkables and the Crown Range in Te Waipounamu South Island to collect seeds and cuttings from alpine buttercups, gentians, forget-me-nots and snow marguerites. These have all been legally collected using Department of Conservation permits.

The native plants grown in the climate-controlled glasshouses include some difficult-to-cultivate alpine beauties such as black scree button daisy, scree buttercup, tall gentian and the white and yellow flowering cushion forget-me-not. There are also cultivated specimens of the rare stalked adder's tongue fern and the beautiful summer pink-flowering ladies' tresses orchid.

The plant collection also serves as an important resource for research, education and conservation purposes. For example, Te Papa botany curator Heidi Meudt has used some of the plants in her research, and the provenance of the specimens is usually well documented.

There are also a few specimens of species that have become extinct in the wild, such as the New Zealand daisy *Celmisia* 'mangaweka', or extinct at a specific location, such as *Gunnera hamiltonii*, a creeping herbaceous plant from the Ōreti River in Southland. This highlights the importance of maintaining a collection as an insurance against extinction in the wild.

Many of our native alpine plant species are declining in the wild, and in some cases disappearing, because of browsing and damage to habitats by deer, possums, hares and tahr. These introduced invasive herbivores are expanding their ranges in the alpine zone as average temperatures

Forget-me-not, *Myosotis exinia*, from Tararua Range.

Ngaio flower.

Ngaio fruits.

Ladies' tresses orchid, *Spiranthes australis*, flowering.

Stalked adder's tongue fern.

Gunnera hamiltonii, one of the rarest native plants in Aotearoa.

The rare leafless *Carmichaelia monroi* stout dwarf broom in flower.

increase, allowing them to reach higher altitudes in summer and remain higher up during winter.

The reserve also has a narrow cave near the pond which has titiwai glow-worms and cave wētā. Some other insects you may see include the kahukōwhai yellow admiral butterfly, New Zealand reticulated stag beetle and New Zealand giant stick insect. Unlike most stick insect species overseas, those in Aotearoa are all flightless. Native fungi recorded here include white basket fungus, earthstars, tawaka mushroom and lilac coral fungus.

GETTING THERE

Catch bus number 150 from Pito One Petone railway station (western end of Jackson Street) or bus number 150 from Lower Hutt, Queensgate (Stop B) to Dowse Drive. From Pito One Petone railway station you can walk to the reserve via the pedestrian overbridge to the western side of State Highway 2 and then to Dowse Drive. There is parking (including disabled) off Dowse Drive (Maungaraki) adjacent to the Dowse interchange on SH2 about 2 kilometres north of Pito One Petone and 2 kilometres south of Lower Hutt CBD. The parking area is locked at dusk.

View from the track, overlooking the river and forest canopy.

24 KAITOKE REGIONAL PARK SWINGBRIDGE TRACK CIRCUIT

This one-hour circuit walk has magnificent views across to a beautiful 1000-year-old lowland podocarp forest with rimu, northern rātā and kahikatea next to the headwaters of Te Awa Kairangi Hutt River. The highlight of a summer visit is to see the northern rātā flowers flaming aloft the canopy of kāmahi, hīnau, miro and black maire.

At Kaitoke you can savour the delicious scent of flowering mākaka native broom alongside the gin-clear river, and relish the lush diversity of native fern species. As you stroll along the track there is also the chance of seeing or hearing smaller forest birds like pōpokotea whitehead, miromiro New Zealand tomtit and pīpīwharauroa shining cuckoo.

You begin the circuit by crossing the swingbridge over the awa from the nearby parking area. Follow the main track up through mature tall rimu and rātā forest with an abundance of ferns and an almost deafening summer cicada chorus. There are two separate lookouts with scenic views over the awa, then soon after that the track drops down to the flume bridge. After crossing the bridge, turn left and continue along the sealed road that takes you back to the parking area where you started.

Walking along this section you pass two small left-hand side tracks off the sealed road that lead down to the awa. The water flows over big greywacke boulders along here. Summer-flowering mākaka flourishes on the opposite bank, and fork ferns grow on the trunks of older tree ferns.

After 'forest bathing', some visitors like to indulge in some river bathing along here during the warmer months. For others, cooling a few bottles in the river is part of their picnic ritual.

There is also a 30-minute Terrace

Forked ferns growing on a tree trunk.

Walk detour off to the right along this section which connects back to the main track. Once you reach the parking area, the nearby Weir Walk offers another 30-minute detour, so there's plenty to explore here. Whatever your plan, you can get a Greater Wellington Regional Council (GWRC) park map online, or in hard copy from the visitor centre near the camping ground. This circuit makes for a nice half- or full-day visit.

The understorey margins of the forest in this part of the park have some attractive native plants, including the dainty white lantern flowers of hīnau; pōkakā; tūrutu New Zealand blueberry; yellow-flowering tarata lemonwood, with

Kihikihi wawā chorus cicada on tree trunk.

Tangle fern.

Perching lilies on tree.

its strongly lemon-scented leaves; and perching tāwhirikaro, which has small, dark reddish-purple flowers. Pikirangi red mistletoe also grows in the vicinity, flowering in November–January. There are also perching lilies and various climbing plants including kiekie, puawānanga native clematis, kareao supplejack and akatawhiwhi scarlet rātā vine.

There is an even greater diversity of native orchid species – 27 in all – in this part of the park than in the Ōtuamotoro Days Bay section of East Harbour Regional Park (EHRP). Notably there are several sun orchids (swamp, striped, toothed), the mountain caps orchid *Caladenia lyallii*, and a variety of *Corybas* spider orchids including *C. hatchii*, *C. oblongus* and *C. rivularis* 'whiskers', which grows by the awa in September–October.

Kaitoke also has a greater diversity of native fern species than the EHRP northern forest (with over 50 in all), and six species of tree fern: mamaku black tree fern, ponga silver fern, whekī-ponga golden tree fern, whekī rough tree fern, kātote soft tree fern and pūnui slender tree fern. Among the many filmy fern species, fan-like filmy fern, rusty filmy fern and hairy filmy fern are notable here. The even greater diversity of ground ferns includes delicate beauties such as the waekura umbrella fern, tangle fern and waewae kākā carrier tangle fern.

Pepeke nguturoa giraffe weevil (male shown here), our longest beetle species, grows up to 9cm.

Striped sun orchid in flower – the blooms only open from about noon to 2pm.

Be on the lookout for kārearea New Zealand falcons and kererū New Zealand pigeons soaring over the awa here, and listen for the loud *zzhweeeesht* calls of koekoeā long-tailed cuckoo in spring and summer, or the mellifluous song of the korimako bellbird chiming out from the surrounding forest. Pīwakawaka New Zealand fantail, riroriro grey warbler and tītitipounamu rifleman are also possible.

The only two reptile species reported in this part of the park are the ngahere gecko and copper skink, but there is a greater diversity among the freshwater fishes, including kōaro, dwarf galaxias, blue-gilled bully and both ōrea long-finned and tuna short-finned eels, plus kōura freshwater crayfish.

The reported insect diversity is not as extensive as at Puketahā, but it's worth watching out for kapokapowai New Zealand bush giant dragonflies, pepeke nguturoa giraffe weevils, pūriri moths and kāmahi green spindle moths.

The carnivorous land snail *Wainuia urnula* is common here, and the unusual 'glow in the dark' freshwater snail (*Latia neritoides*) that lives in the streams is thought to be the world's only bioluminescent freshwater creature.

There are longer tracks to explore in the park, including the 3–4-hour Ridge Track, which connects to Te Mārua pumping station.

Rusty filmy ferns growing on tree trunk.

GETTING THERE

The nearest bus stop to the swingbridge car park is 8 kilometres away. The number 112 bus from Upper Hutt railway station stops at Te Marua Stores on Plateau Road. Even if you take your bike with you on the bus and then cycle from Te Mārua it is still a long return cycle along a very busy road, so until there is a better public transport option this site is best visited by car or electric vehicle. It is 16 kilometres from Upper Hutt railway station to the swingbridge car park in the park, which is about a 20-minute drive.

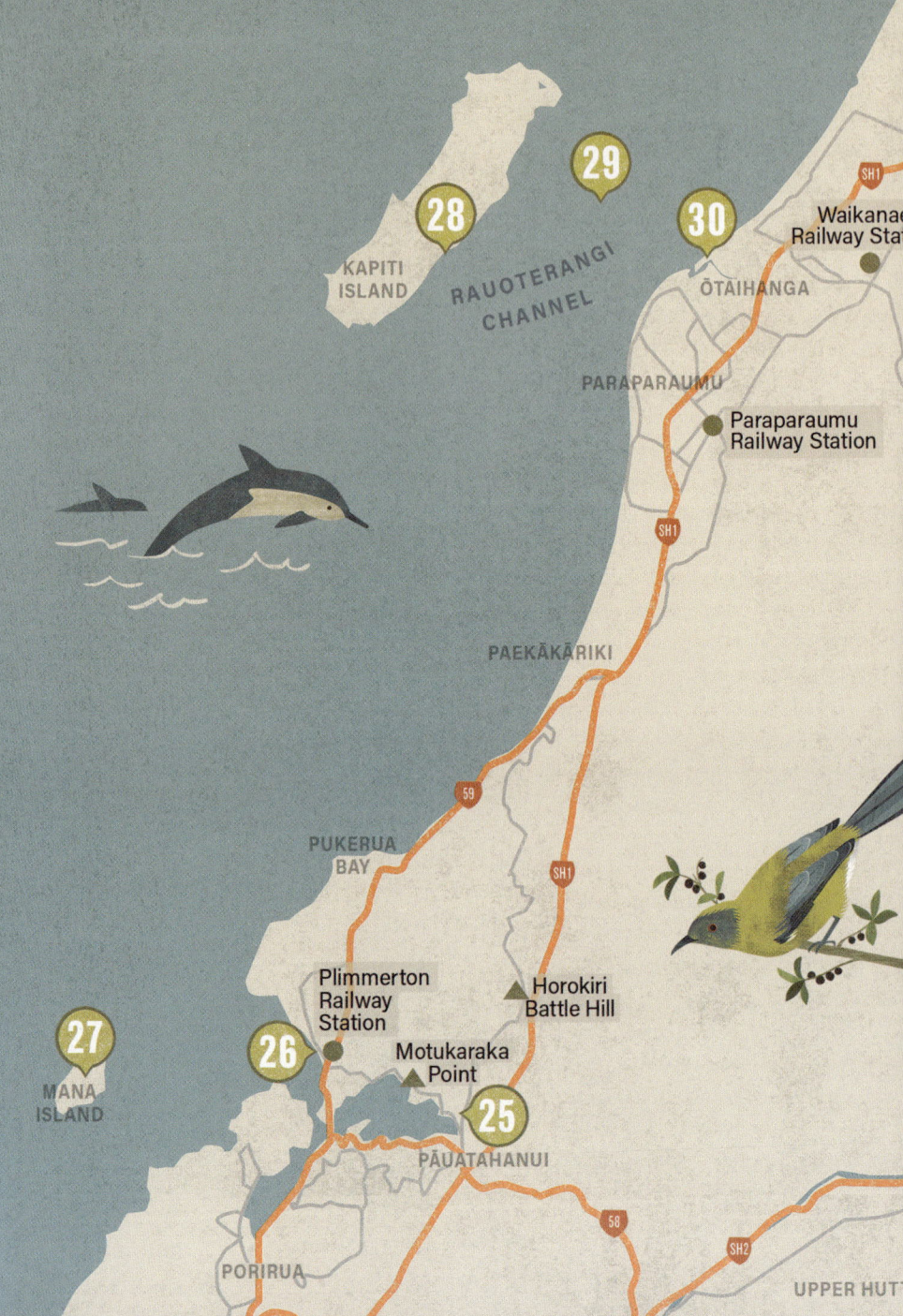

MAI TE AWARUA-O-PORIRUA KI ŌTAIHANGA
PORIRUA AND KAPITI COAST

He whānau, he whenua: Connecting whānau and whenua	215
25. Pāuatahanui Wildlife Reserve	218
26. Plimmerton Beach and foreshore	224
27. Mana Island Scientific Reserve	230
28. Kapiti Island Nature Reserve	236
29. Kapiti Marine Reserve	242
30. Waikanae Estuary Scientific Reserve	246

Ngāti Toa, and the representative iwi authority, Te Rūnanga o Toa Rangatira, acknowledge and affirm our responsibility to uphold the mana prestige, rangatiratanga sovereignty and mauri life force of the whenua land, wai water, natural resources and people within the rohe district as consistent with the kawa protocols, tikanga customs and mātāpono principles of Ngāti Toa.

During the Ngāti Toa heke migration of the early 1800s from Kāwhia, Kapiti Island was recognised as a key strategic asset due to its proximity to the mainland and the ability to defend it in times of conflict. Maintaining mana over the island was a key reason why Ngāti Toa was able to establish its presence in Te Upoko-o-Te-Ika southern North Island as well as in Te Tauihu-o-Te-Waka-a-Māui the top of the South Island, given the conflict that existed during the development of tribal alliances.

In contemporary times, Kapiti Island has become a key conservation estate with many native species now able to thrive due to its pest-free status. Ngāti Toa continues to value its strategic and contemporary significance and maintains strong ties to the island through partnerships and relationships with the Department of Conservation and other key government organisations. The Ngāti Toa Rangatira Claims Settlement Act 2014 also provides a platform for meaningful and authentic connections to Kapiti and other sites in our rohe, some of which are included in the following pages.

The Barrett whānau hold an ahikā cultural occupation role on Kapiti Island and they maintain a close and intimate connection to the island, just one example of how our people are reaffirming their kaitiakitanga. This is their story.

Rawiri Faulkner, Pou Toa Matarau, Te Rūnanga o Toa Rangatira

The following story has been adapted from an article by Lee-Anne Duncan in the January/February 2019 issue of *NZ Life & Leisure*.

HE WHĀNAU, HE WHENUA: CONNECTING WHĀNAU AND WHENUA

The vast majority of Kapiti Island is a nature reserve. But 20 hectares of the iconic island is privately owned by a whānau dedicated to preserving their whakapapa – including the land and everything upon it – and sharing it with the world. The Barrett whānau are among the descendants who remain on the island as guardians of this bird-lover's paradise and Kapiti Island Nature Tours lodge.

The island, one of New Zealand's most accessible nature reserves, is a vivid and vocal example of what investing in eradicating pests can achieve. The list of resident native birds is extensive, the dawn chorus is raucous and roly-poly kererū are confident enough to feed on the ground.

John Barrett and his wife Sue and sister Amo Clark have built up Kapiti Island Nature Tours over the past two decades on land towards the north end of the island. 'When we set up Kapiti Island Nature Tours, the whole kaupapa was to provide an opportunity for the whānau to do something positive and productive for ourselves,' says John. 'What's happened over the past 20 years is that we've become stronger with our whakapapa, and stronger in providing a Māori/conservation/soft-adventure tourism product. We want to be developing something that's great, not just good – something that people talk about and that enhances the mana of our whānau, hapū, iwi and district.' Kapiti Island fair looms over the coast that shares its name. So perhaps it's surprising how many locals have never made the trip. But Ōtaki-born-and-bred Sue understands. 'Kapiti Island is very spiritual for a lot of people in the area and some, I think, feel if they came it might spoil the feeling they have of it.'

Sue also has a whānau connection as her grandparents farmed at Rangatira, at the mid-point of the island, back before the government bought the island

– bar the Barretts' bit – and decreed it a nature reserve in 1892. As the bush regenerated around them, John's whānau continued to farm their piece of the island until 1966, doggedly resisting government pressure to hand over their land. After John's uncle left the farm in 1966, no one regularly came to the island until John and Sue started building their bach in 1975.

'We can't improve on the natural aspects of the island,' says John. 'The bush regeneration is taking place at a fantastic rate. Since we've been here, we've seen the bush grow down the valley towards us, we hear kōkako up the valley, and we have tīeke saddlebacks here and takahē wandering around the lodge. It just feels good to be here. And as I've become older, the rationale becomes clearer; that it's to do with wider whānau connections, it's about our great-grandparents and the whole whakapapa.'

Kapiti Island's human story goes back hundreds of years, but the Barretts' began in the 1820s. 'There were two main waves of migration around then, by sea and hīkoi, when tribes from Ngāti Toa, Te Āti Awa and Ngāti Raukawa came from Waikato and Taranaki,' says John, a direct descendant of that migration. They were led by Te Rauparaha, the famed and feared Ngāti Toa chief who swept down the west coast of Aotearoa after being forced out of Waikato. But the Barretts trace their whakapapa to another warrior who travelled with him, Te Rangihīroa. Over the next 20 years, the area was settled by whalers and sealers, followed by traders and farmers. Then, in 1840, the Taranaki tribes left Kapiti to return to fight in the land wars going on in their home region. 'We have this land because Te Rangihīroa's mother, Metapere Waipunāhau – my granny's grandma – and a few other families were left behind to look after it,' says John.

John says the whānau enjoys a 'respectful and collaborative' relationship with the Department of Conservation and its staff who visit, tracking the area's fauna and flora. 'DOC has an obligation to the Treaty of Waitangi in its legislation. It's happy to exercise that obligation and allow us to keep our part of the island.' Back in the 1980s, John and Sue ran a ten-week residential programme for 17- to 25-year-olds. 'It was a mix of recreation, education and conservation,' says John. 'Then we had parents asking if they could come and stay, then friends of parents, then friends of friends.' When the programme's funding stopped in the mid-1990s, Kapiti Island Nature Tours began.

These days, John and Sue's son Manaaki Barrett has taken over a lot of the business operation. 'The longer I stay here, and the more I see how other indigenous people around the world lack an opportunity to connect to their place and to share it, I see that what we have is pretty special. We're here talking about our history every day so our connection with our culture and our whakapapa is enhanced and cemented,' says Manaaki. 'If I'd stayed in the city, working in an office, the path I took to reconnect with my whakapapa and culture would have been slower. Being here in the same place as my great-great-great-great grandfather is a powerful way of connecting with that.'

Kiwi pukupuku little spotted kiwi live around the lodge, leaving their burrows to forage in the dark. In theory, night-time kiwi-spotting should be easy as kiwi are surprisingly noisy. They call from the bush, the male's chirrup pitching higher in intensity as he strains for a female's reply. 'Sometimes they walk right through the group, even brushing through our legs,' says Manaaki. 'If you get up during the night, take care because you're quite likely to see them round your cabins.'

Elsewhere ruru hoot, kākā screech, kororā flap, weka call and wētā scrape their hind legs. In the dark of the bush, there might not always be much to see but there's plenty to hear. The island has to be one of the best places to gaze at the night sky, search for kiwi, and try to identify bird calls. But invertebrates and lizards have also thrived since pests were eradicated in 1996, including the common gecko, which likes to hide in the seats of the visitors' shelter.

Manaaki says most visitors are interested in Kapiti Island's human story and the majority are New Zealanders. 'People genuinely get a lot out of their experience here. So it's quite a nourishing thing for us to put our efforts into facilitating that experience, helping our manuhiri get the best out of Kapiti.' Sue adds, 'If, as a family, we can build a business around our presence here that will sustain our land, our whakapapa, and connect us with our tūrangawaewae while sharing that with visitors then I'm in.'

View of one of the ponds in the reserve.

25 PĀUATAHANUI WILDLIFE RESERVE

If you want to see big skies reflected in freshwater ponds with warou welcome swallows and kapokapowai dragonflies zooming around white-faced herons, then Pāuatahanui Wildlife Reserve on a sunny summer day is the place to go. This 50-hectare Department of Conservation reserve includes a 4-hectare Forest & Bird reserve and contains the most significant coastal salt-marsh habitat in the southern part of the motu.

This reserve is located at the east end of Pāuatahanui Inlet, one of two arms of Te Awarua-o-Porirua Harbour, which is the largest estuarine ecosystem in southern Te Ika-a-Māui North Island. The inlet is deep enough for maki orca to swim in it, as a pod of seven did in late August 2021 and a pod of three in late September 2023.

The reserve is an important staging post for wading birds migrating between Te Waipounamu South Island and Te Ika-a-Māui North Island, such as tōrea South Island pied oystercatcher and kuaka bar-tailed godwit. The varied habitats here also support a healthy diversity of resident bird species. A total of 35 species have been regularly observed by Birds New Zealand surveys.

Among the most commonly seen wading birds are the balletic poaka pied stilt, raucous spur-winged plover and charming pohowera banded dotterel. The waterfowl include pūtangitangi paradise shelducks and tētē grey teal, and both

Poaka pied stilt pair.

kāhu swamp harriers and kōtare sacred kingfishers are seen here too.

Kōtuku ngutupapa royal spoonbills visit the reserve to feed. Their big black, spoon-shaped bill is unmistakable. In breeding plumage, they have long white crest feathers on the back of the head, a creamy-yellow breast, a yellow patch above each red eye and a red patch in the middle of the forehead. Watch for them feeding while wading in the shallows, scything their submerged bill to catch small fish and shrimps. They are able to detect vibrations inside their bill, which allows them to find their prey in muddy water or at night. Then they snap their bill shut and lift it up so the prey slides down their throat.

Elegant bluish-grey white-faced herons stalk the wetlands and mud flats on their long yellow legs hunting for small

Tētē grey teal pair.

Kāhu swamp harrier gliding overhead.

Moho pererū banded rail.

The iconic pūkeko is an abundant, smaller relative of the takahē.

The spur-winged plover is named for the two yellow 'spurs' on its wings.

fish and crabs with their long, dark spear bill. If you see one in summer, check out the long grey, strap-like plumes on its back and shorter pinkish-brown plumes on its front. It raises and fans out these plumes during courtship displays. Watch also for the graceful symmetry of herons and poaka reflected in the still waters of the ponds. Both have long legs, but stilts have the longest legs relative to their body size among all birds. Pohowera stalk for small crabs and worms on the mud flats, and there are a few reports of tūturiwhatu New Zealand dotterels here, too.

The reserve is a hot spot for the cheeky pūkeko. Its deep blue-violet plumage, bright red bill and orange legs make it hard to miss. A smaller cousin of the takahē, it lives in permanent groups that defend a shared territory and have a fascinating breeding ecology. Pūkeko nest in monogamous pairs, sometimes with an extra male or an extra female, and sometimes with non-breeding helpers. When multiple breeding females are present, they lay in the same nest. The clutch usually contains four to six large speckled, pale cream-coloured eggs per female, and when all the females in the group use the same nest, they can lay up to 18 eggs. Breeding males incubate the eggs with help from the breeding females, and all the group members care for the young.

The black fluffy chicks are a favoured prey of the native kāhu swamp harrier, the largest of the world's 16 harrier species. In flight, kāhu often glide, holding their long wings in a shallow V-shape with tips upturned. Watch also for the kāhu's dramatic 'sky dancing' courtship displays, in which it makes impressive repeated dives and sharp upward swoops.

Less visible are the resident pūweto spotless crakes. Listen out for the bubbling and trilling 'lawnmower' calls of the pūweto, or its short *pit-pit* and *mook-mook* calls. Watch for it stalking along the edge of the reeds or furtively walking out onto exposed muddy areas, where it picks up small insects and worms. This very small, sooty grey and brown rail with a brief black bill and long pinkish legs is not often seen in the open, but in summer it sometimes leads its black fluffy chicks to feed on the muddy margins of the ponds.

The moho pererū banded rail has also been recorded here. This medium-sized rail looks like a pocket weka with an intricately white-barred black front. Like its larger cousin it is well camouflaged, but not as bold. This bird prefers staying inside its marshy comfort zone, but is sometimes seen walking out onto the mud to feed on crabs and snails as the tide recedes. The best time to look for it is January–February.

Mātātā fernbirds were reintroduced at the reserve in 2017, so be sure to listen for their *u-tick u-tick* calls and watch for them perched on reed stems, or flying between clumps of vegetation when you may glimpse their tatty long tail feathers, chestnut crown, and speckled breast. They mostly creep mouse-like through the reeds but are sometimes visible at the edge of the reed beds as they glean small insects.

The saltmarshes offer a chance to see the small yellow flowers of bachelor's button alongside the estuary in May–October, and the white and pink flowers of māakoako sea primrose in December. The warmth of summer coaxes out blue-spotted hawkers, ranger dragonflies and red damselflies, which zoom around chasing after the same small flying insects as the warou welcome swallows. Warou will also catch juvenile damselflies.

The reserve's five wooden bird hides provide close viewing opportunities, each within 500 metres of the start of the red track and blue track, which start near Paekākāriki Hill Road, and the green track, which starts from Grays Road. Four of the hides overlook freshwater ponds, while the fifth overlooks the tidal mudflats, where there is a handy kawau shag roost site. All the tracks are flat with wheelchair access.

GETTING THERE

The number 236 bus route runs from Porirua and Paremata railway stations to Joseph Banks Drive. The bus stop at The Masthead near 51 Joseph Banks Drive is a kilometre from the reserve entrance off Paekākāriki Hill Road. There is parking near that entrance and at Grays Road near the intersection with Paekākāriki Hill Road.

Māakoako sea primrose in flower.

Pūweto spotless crake foraging by a reed bed.

Mātātā fernbird foraging by a reed bed.

Ranger dragonfly.

Blue-spotted hawker on a reed stem.

View from Plimmerton fire station rocks out to sea, with a flock of tara white-fronted terns.

26 PLIMMERTON BEACH AND FORESHORE

This scenic 3-kilometre return walk alongside the rocky foreshore and sandy beaches of Plimmerton has panoramic sea views west to Mana Island and south-west to Whitireia Park Reserve. The coastline here supports a good diversity of coastal birds, and in recent years it has gained a reputation among birdwatchers and photographers as a 'hot spot' for terns.

Eurasian common tern in breeding plumage.

Sooty tern in breeding plumage.

The local tara white-fronted tern flock that gathers here in summer and autumn is the main drawcard. This consists mostly of birds from the nearby breeding colony on Mana Island, although some from Waikanae and Kapiti Island also find their way here when food availability and wind direction are favourable. Taranui Caspian terns and tarapirohe black-fronted terns also sometimes roost with the tara flock.

In February 2022, the tara flock was also joined by a few Eurasian common terns, a tropical sooty tern and the first record of a Eurasian black tern in Aotearoa, much to the delight of local birdwatchers. At the time, the tara flock was regularly seen on coastal rocks behind the small Plimmerton fire station building, and on publicly accessible coastal rocks behind 7A Moana Road, usually around high tide. This was an opportunity to visit both locations for closer views of the rarer terns among the flock.

Other birds that often gather on the rocks along here are karoro southern black-backed gull, tarāpunga red-billed gulls, kawau shags, tōrea pango variable oystercatchers and the occasional white-faced heron or matuku moana reef heron.

The native karoro is one of the largest of all gull species, growing up to 60 centimetres and weighing up to a kilogram, but it can be a confusing species to identify. The adult bird has a white head and body, black back, chunky yellow bill with a red spot by the tip, and pale greenish legs. In contrast, the juvenile is dark mottled brown-grey with black bill and legs. Its plumage gets paler as it gets older, and the bill becomes pale pink until it reaches adult plumage at three years old and the bill becomes yellow. The species is widespread in Aotearoa, with a breeding range that extends as far south as Mauka Huka the Subantarctic Islands.

Kāruhiruhi pied shags and kawaupaka little pied shags are the most abundant

Kawau tūī little black shag – one of 12 shag species that breed in Aotearoa.

Adult kawaupaka little pied shag – Aotearoa has more shag species than any other country.

shags here. The kāruhiruhi is a striking, rather slim white-fronted black shag with a long, pale, hooked bill, vivid blue eye rings, green eyes and yellow facial skin. The smaller kawaupaka has a shorter yellow bill, a long tail, brown eyes and variable plumage. Most adults are black with white cheeks and throat, or black with completely white underparts, or intermediate, and all develop a head crest during the breeding season.

Kawau tūī little black shags also do quite well here, with fast-moving flocks of up to 50 sometimes seen feeding in the water between the fire station rocks and the marina. If you see these snake-headed black birds roosting by the marina, check out their striking turquoise-green eyes. Kawau tūī, kāruhiruhi and kawaupaka all have black legs and feet.

Wading birds sometimes make an appearance on the fire station rocks and local beaches, including spur-winged plover, poaka pied stilt and kuaka bar-tailed godwit. Tākapu Australasian gannets and kōtuku ngutupapa royal spoonbills are most likely to be seen flying past the rocks heading towards Pāuatahanui Inlet, and flocks of pakahā fluttering shearwaters sometimes feed offshore. When they do, they are often joined by tara – and when that happens, check for Arctic skuas chasing after the tara.

The Plimmerton Boating Club marina sometimes has a tara flock, too, and is visited by kawau shags, tōrea

Adult karoro southern black-backed gull.

pango variable oystercatchers and matuku moana reef herons. Adding to Plimmerton's reputation as a hot spot for terns was the Arctic tern seen at the marina with the tara flock in May 2016. This species nests in Arctic regions of the northern hemisphere and makes the longest annual migration of any bird species, flying up to 90,000 kilometres every year from the Arctic to Antarctica, where it feeds near the pack-ice edge before returning to breed at its northern breeding grounds. It can live for up to 30 years; so over a lifetime, one can fly the equivalent distance from the Earth to the Moon and back more than three times. Although there are two million Arctic terns, they are only rarely found in Aotearoa.

Kekeno New Zealand fur seals sometimes haul out along the Plimmerton coast in winter and spring, so it's not surprising that this area also has a history of rare seal sightings. A rāpoka leopard seal from Antarctica hauled out on Plimmerton Beach in late September 2016 and was seen again on nearby Tītahi Bay beach a few days later. A young subantarctic fur seal was found on Tītahi Bay beach on 23 June 2015, and a 1.5-metre juvenile Weddell seal from Antarctica was found on the same beach on 26 June 1926. So if you see a seal hauled out along here, it is worth taking photos and checking which species it is.

Pods of aihe common dolphins pass along the Plimmerton coast fairly regularly, and pods of maki orca are occasionally seen heading towards Pāuatahanui Inlet and Porirua Harbour. A pod of seven maki were seen regularly on the Plimmerton coast and in Pāuatahanui Inlet from 28 August to 1 September 2021. When another pod passed the Plimmerton coast on 11 July 2021, a young calf became stranded among some rocks. The Department of Conservation and local volunteers moved it to the nearby marina boat ramp, where the water was penned off and it was cared for in the hope that its pod would return, but it died on 23 July.

A rare Arnoux's beaked whale was photographed breaching off Tītahi Bay on 6 February 2021, and a rare Shepherd's beaked whale was found dead on Tītahi Bay beach on 19 September 2014, so keep an eye out for unusual-looking whales off the coast here. It's also worth watching out for carpet sharks, whai keo eagle rays and koinga rig houndsharks, which are sometimes seen in shallow inshore waters during summer.

The bright white shells of the paper nautilus, a form of pelagic octopus, sometimes wash up in this area. Among the other interesting shells to look out for on the beaches are the common fan scallop, Arabic volute, Cook's turban, heavy-ribbed venus, turret shell and spotted tiger topshell. A rich diversity of sponges and seaweeds often wash up after storms, another sign of a healthy inshore seafloor ecosystem.

GETTING THERE

Regular trains run to Plimmerton from Wellington station and the Kapiti Coast. From Plimmerton station, walk or cycle north past the nearby shops and then along the coastal path that passes the fire station along Moana Road to the Plimmerton Boating Club marina. There is parking by the shops, the fire station and the marina, and the coastal footpath is suitable for wheelchairs.

The kāruhiruhi pied shag has vivid blue eye rings and yellow facial skin in the breeding season.

View of Mana Island from Plimmerton fire station rocks.

27 MANA ISLAND SCIENTIFIC RESERVE

Mana Island is a textbook ecological restoration success story where visitors can see a wide range of rare or threatened endemic species. Since the 1980s it has gone from being a grassy livestock farm to a forested island that ranks as one of the key sites for takahē conservation outside of Te Rua-o-Te-Moko Fiordland, and the world's most complex seabird translocation project.

The Department of Conservation (DOC) released the first takahē here in 1988, two years after the last cattle were taken off and three years before Mana Island was declared pest-free. The takahē population grew to 42 by 2007 and until recently was the largest outside of Fiordland. Between 1989 and 2022, a total of 91 takahē were translocated from the island to other sites. The current population is seven or eight pairs, with birds most often seen in the grassy area around the DOC buildings near the landing area.

Since 1997, three seabird species have been translocated to artificial burrows above the south-west coast of the island. Pakahā fluttering shearwater, kuaka common diving petrel and tītī wainui fairy prion chicks were taken from existing colonies in the Marlborough Sounds and off the Taranaki coast and placed in artificial burrows on Mana Island, where they were hand-fed sardine smoothies or krill until they fledged. Some of these survived to adulthood and have since returned to breed here themselves.

According to Te Papa vertebrates curator Colin Miskelly, who was closely involved in all three translocations, the main aim was to restore the birds' role as 'ecosystem engineers', depositing marine nutrients on the island and improving habitat quality for native reptiles and insects by digging burrows. These translocations also helped with

Returning kuaka common diving petrel on Mana Island, October 2014.

developing new techniques that were subsequently applied elsewhere to other, more threatened seabird species. Along with another of Te Papa's vertebrates curators, Alan Tennyson, and Te Papa genomic researcher Lara Shepherd, Colin Miskelly has published extensively on the seabirds of Aotearoa, including describing new species.

After the success of the takahē translocations, 20 juvenile rowi Ōkarito brown kiwi were released here in 2012. Once these large, long-billed brown kiwi started breeding, surplus juveniles were removed to establish a new wild population south of Ōkarito in the

Moko pāpā Raukawa gecko can live for as long as 20 years.

Rowi Ōkarito brown kiwi have a maximum lifespan of 34 to 48 years.

Omoeroa Range of Te Waipounamu. Rowi are now present all over the island – but since they are nocturnal, don't expect to see them during a daytime visit.

Pāteke brown teal, yellow-crowned kākāriki, toutouwai North Island robin, mātātā fernbird, pōpokotea whitehead and korimako bellbird have also been successfully translocated here since 1995. They are now dispersed around the whole island, with pāteke mostly seen in the Waikōkō wetland area. Mātātā are abundant in shrubland on the plateau, while the other species are in both the regenerating forest and shrubland. A few species have returned on their own to breed here, including tūī, pūkeko and kāruhiruhi pied shag, while kererū New Zealand pigeons and kārearea New Zealand falcons are regular visitors, and ruru moreporks are sometimes present in low numbers.

Mana Island is also an important breeding site for the feisty kororā little blue penguin, whose natural wild population nests near the landing area and along the coast. There is also a natural breeding population of tītī sooty shearwaters. Tara white-fronted terns and tarāpunga red-billed gulls breed at the north end of the island, and a few interesting seabirds are sometimes seen from the ferry including pakahā fluttering shearwaters and Arctic skuas, which often chase after terns and gulls at sea.

Prior to becoming a scientific reserve,

Flax weevil.

the island supported six reptile species: moko pāpā Raukawa gecko, moko mangaeka goldstripe gecko, mokomoko northern grass skink, glossy brown skink, McGregor's skink and copper skink. Five more have been translocated here since 1998: moko kākāriki barking gecko, Tohu's gecko, ngahere gecko, kōkōwai northern spotted skink and Newman's speckled skink. Of these, moko pāpā, mokomoko and copper skink are now very abundant and are the most likely to be seen by visitors to our most bedragoned isle. Their glistening scales can often be seen in the coastal zone near the landing area and by grassy track edges on still, sunny days.

Populations of Cook Strait giant wētā and Wellington tree wētā have both survived on the island, while the large flightless flax weevil and Hutton's speargrass weevil were translocated here between 2004 and 2007.

Since 1998, the Friends of Mana Island (FOMI) volunteer group has taken the

View of native plantings looking across to Mākara wind farm.

lead role in most conservation initiatives here, in partnership with mana whenua Ngāti Toa Rangatira and DOC. The wider ecological restoration programme has been a three-way partnership between government (DOC), mana whenua and the wider community, with thousands of people contributing their time and mahi. A few other community groups have also organised conservation projects here, most notably Wellington Botanical Society, Forest & Bird and Birds New Zealand.

Since 1987, DOC and other groups have planted a diverse range of nearly half a million native plants and trees, ranging from nīkau, tītoki and kohekohe to māhoe, wharariki coastal flax and nau Cook's scurvy grass. Most of the island is now cloaked in coastal broadleaved forest, shrubland or flaxland.

From Plimmerton, the island looks like a natural fortress rising out of the shimmering sea. It is about 3 kilometres by 2 kilometres, with steep 120-metre cliffs

Mokomoko northern grass skink.

Immature takahē - this is the largest living rail species in the world.

along much of its coast. Visitors arrive by ferry on the south-east coast, at a shingle beach next to a level area of scrub and shrubland with various DOC buildings. A network of tracks fans out from here, the main one being the Tirohanga Track, which makes a circuit around most of the island. All guided walks are anticlockwise, and the numbered posts for self-guided walks are arranged for an anticlockwise circuit that starts by heading north from the assembly point by the old woolshed. On clear days, where the Tirohanga Track runs along the tops, there are stunning views of Te Waipounamu. Download the track map from DOC's website or get a hard copy from the DOC office in Wellington.

GETTING THERE

No permit is required to visit, so if visiting privately you can go there by yacht or motor boat at any time of the year, but you must anchor offshore and transfer yourself. Do not take dogs. Alternatively, the Go Mana ferry service departs from Mana marina near Mana railway station. Visitors delivered by Go Mana can explore the island on their own except during the October–December period, when all trips must be fully guided due to the takahē breeding programme. There is parking by Mana station.

View of Kapiti Island from Paraparaumu Beach.

28 KAPITI ISLAND NATURE RESERVE

Visitors to Kapiti Island can see some of our most threatened endemic bird species in tall native forest at one of the oldest and most important nature reserves in Aotearoa. This taonga island towers up to 521 metres above sea level where the Wilkinson Track rises to a viewing platform with spectacular views of the Kapiti Coast and Te Waipounamu South Island.

In the late nineteenth century, the first legally protected nature reserves in Aotearoa were created at Te Hauturu-o-Toi Little Barrier Island, Tau Moana Resolution Island and Kapiti Island. Sadly, a planned translocation of the huia to Kapiti Island in the 1890s did not eventuate before the species became extinct in 1907. The mātuhituhi bush wren was last reported on Kapiti island on 31 March 1911, but was wiped out here by invasive introduced predators soon after that and is now also extinct.

The prospects for conservation success here dramatically improved once this 2000-hectare island was declared predator-free in 1998. Since then, 12 native bird species have been translocated or released here, including kiwi pukupuku little spotted kiwi, North Island kōkako, weka, hihi stitchbird, tīeke saddleback and pāteke brown teal.

Natural populations of kororā little blue penguin, pōpokotea whitehead, toutouwai North Island robin, ruru morepork and tītī sooty shearwater have survived and breed here. The two migrant cuckoos – koekoeā long-tailed cuckoo and pīpīwharauroa shining cuckoo – breed here, and both kārearea New Zealand falcon and kāhu swamp harrier are regularly seen patrolling over the forest canopy.

This is the only place in the Te Upoko-o-te-Ika area where you can see North Island kōkako and weka, and one of the best wild places in the country to see and hear kiwi pukupuku. Kapiti Island has the largest population of kiwi pukupuku, with over 1600 birds. It is possible to book with Kapiti Island Nature Tours to stay overnight in private accommodation at the north end of the island, where kiwi can be seen after dark. Listen for their ascending whistles and trills, or the snuffling sound of one clearing its nostrils between probing for worms.

Kōkako are most often seen up the Wilkinson and Trig tracks. There are now over 50 pairs nesting on the island, and they are increasingly being seen lower down by the Rangatira Loop Track area, and even by the Rangatira flat itself, as their numbers grow. For example, I saw a pair building a nest in the vicinity of Rangatira flat in summer 2022/23. These blue-wattled beauties have one of the longest duet song performances of any songbird. Listen for their sublime

Kōkako perched in kohekohe.

Tītī sooty shearwater.

Pūriri trunk with northern rātā vine.

Male hihi stitchbird – the te reo name means 'ray of sunlight'.

Koekoeā long-tailed cuckoo.

Weka adult.

Weka chick.

haunting song of sustained, organ-like notes, which evokes the ancient forests of Aotearoa, and watch for them feeding on the ripe red fruits of tītoki and nīkau.

Another specialty bird here is the three-toed koekoeā, which breeds in November–December by parasitising the nests of pōpokotea. The best way to search for this cryptic bird is to listen for its loud, shrieking *zzhweeeesht* calls. If you hear one nearby, try to scan the area with binoculars and watch for any movement. The section of the Wilkinson Track above the first feeder is a good area to look for it. Another strategy is to watch the forest canopy from in front of the whare on Rangatira flat, scanning the treetops in the hope that you will see one fly up and over the forest canopy. Smaller-bodied and longer-tailed than the similar-looking kārearea, this distinctly wary bird makes the longest annual migration over water of any forest bird species, flying up to 6500 kilometres from eastern Polynesia to Aotearoa to breed in early summer, and then all the way back again a few months later.

Weka now thrive on the island so are often seen walking around near the

Ngahere gecko head.

Ngahere gecko.

landing area, by the forest tracks and near the feeders. These big, brown-streaked and red-billed flightless rails often have a couple of juveniles with them in summer. Famously inquisitive snatchers of food and objects, they will check out any bag left on the ground. Takahē, tīeke, kākā and red-crowned kākāriki also breed here and are regularly seen in the Rangatira flat and nearby lower track area.

Tīeke are usually seen bounding vigorously around the forest or on the ground in the same area, but hihi are mostly seen near the feeders along the Wilkinson and Trig tracks, where they can be heard making their high-pitched *titch* calls. Kākā are most often seen flying over the forest canopy or perched in trees near the whare, while toutouwai can usually be seen along any of the forested tracks, both near Rangatira flat and at the north end of the island.

Along with Mana and Matiu Somes, Kapiti is an important breeding site for kororā, which nest all around the coast of the island. Tara white-fronted terns sometimes breed on the coast at the north end. Also at the north end, Ōkupe Lagoon is a refuge for pāpango New Zealand scaup, pāteke brown teal and kuruwhengi Australasian shoveler, and has a growing kōtuku ngutupapa royal spoonbill colony. Birds from here fly over to feed at Waikanae Estuary and Pāuatahanui Inlet.

The island's original forest was mostly northern rātā and podocarps such as mataī and miro. Some of these big old trees have survived in the deep gullies, but the main forests here today are kohekohe, tawa and kānuka, and large areas are covered in regenerating scrub dominated by whauwhaupaku five-finger and māhoe.

A few native orchid species grow by the Wilkinson Track during the warmer months, such as maikuku common sun orchid, tutukiwi greenhood orchid and hūperei black orchid. Winter greenhood orchids and pixie cap orchids also grow here in winter. The tree ferns here include mamaku black tree fern, kātote soft tree fern and pūnui slender tree fern, and the ground ferns include pākau gully fern, huruhuru whenua shining spleenwort and kōwaowao hound's tongue fern.

The island also has a good diversity of reintroduced reptiles, with moko pāpā Raukawa gecko, the mokopirirakau form of ngahere gecko, moko kākāriki barking gecko and moko mangaeka goldstripe gecko, plus ornate skink, copper skink and mokomoko northern grass skink. Watch for skinks by the Rangatira flat tracks and going up Wilkinson Track to the first feeder. Geckos are sometimes seen in the gaps between the timber slats of the whare on Rangatira flat.

There are some interesting winged insects, including the pūriri moth, pepe para riki North Island coastal copper butterfly and kahukura red admiral butterfly. Among the ground insects, watch for the pepeke nguturoa giraffe weevil, blackish meadow katydid, prickly stick insect and stinking ground beetle. The bright white shells of paper nautilus also wash up on the beach from time to time.

Since 2015 the Kapiti Island Strategic Advisory Committee, comprising Ngāti Toa Rangatira and Department of Conservation representatives, has guided the future management of the island to ensure an integrated approach to knowledge and learning combining mātauranga Māori and western science, and increased participation for Ngāti Toa iwi members in kaitiakitanga of Kapiti Island. It also has oversight of the preparation and approval of a conservation management plan for the Kapiti Island Reserve sites, as provided for in the Ngāti Toa Treaty of Waitangi Settlement of 2014.

GETTING THERE

A return ferry service operated by Kapiti Island Nature Tours departs from the Kapiti Boating Club at Paraparaumu Beach and drops visitors at Rangatira flat and the north end. The number 262 bus connects Paraparaumu railway station and Paraparaumu Beach, and there is a train service to Paraparaumu station from Wellington and Waikanae. Kapiti Island Nature Tours also offer overnight private accommodation and guided walks at the north end. DOC volunteers usually stay in the small cottages by Rangatira flat. The ferry ticket price includes the DOC permit required to land on the island.

View of the marine reserve area across to Kapiti Island.

29 KAPITI MARINE RESERVE

The Kapiti Marine Reserve was established in 1992 and covers about 20 square kilometres in two separate areas adjacent to the island. After three decades of being a no-take zone, previously targeted species, such as kōura rock lobster, tāmure snapper, pākirikiri blue cod and black-foot pāua, are now recovering here.

There is an abundance of marine wildlife, such as kororā little blue penguins, kekeno New Zealand fur seals and aihe common dolphins, in and around the reserve area, and a wealth of imaginatively named sea creatures are found within it, such as carpet shark, bearded rock cod, āhuruhuru goatfish, white-spotted dogfish and blanket octopus.

The 3-square-kilometre western portion of the marine reserve extends along the north-west side of the island about a kilometre out to sea, while the larger 18-square-kilometre eastern part extends about 4 kilometres along the upper north-east coast of the island and about 6 kilometres across to a 1-kilometre strip of the coast at Waikanae Estuary Scientific Reserve. Although the east coast of the island is sheltered from westerly winds, it has strong tidal currents.

The sheltered reefs and sandy seabed support a rich variety of marine life, from colourful sea sponges, pātangatanga sea stars and sea anemones to whai keo eagle rays and reef fish such as banded wrasse.

There is good snorkelling and scuba diving off the island in Hole-in-the-Wall Bay and around Arapawaiti Point along the northernmost part of the island. The reefs from Hole-in-the-Wall Bay to Trig Point have rimurapa kelp forests, which are a haven for tāmure snapper, red moki, wheke octopus and kōura rock lobster. The deeper rocky reefs have sponge gardens with butterfly perch and banded perch. In summer, haku yellowtail kingfish feed on the resident fish, and taha pounamu blue sharks are sometimes seen swimming through the reserve.

The island is also an important reef off what is otherwise a very long stretch of sandy mainland coast. A number of warmer-water stragglers have been seen here, such as the Australian silverspot, magpie perch and spotted sawtail.

The rocky reefs on the eastern coast from Whakahoua to Waterfall Bay have plenty of marine life for divers to discover. Wheke, kōura and whai keo live here, and the fish life includes spotties, āhuruhuru and silver drummer. Blanket octopus are also present, and paper nautilus, a pelagic octopus, is sometimes seen in the water. A shallow-water black coral colony in the vicinity of the marine reserve, thought to be hundreds of years old, is the same species as that found growing in the fiords of Te Rua-o-te-moko Fiordland.

Red moki.

Aihe common dolphins.

Tara white-fronted tern.

There is a winter kekeno New Zealand fur seal haul-out at Arapawaiti Point, and aihe common dolphins are often seen in the reserve area during spring and summer. There was a rare sighting of two tutumairekurai Hector's dolphins from a boat travelling between Kapiti Island and the mainland on 11 October 2023, and maki orca, tohorā southern right whales and paikea humpback whales are sometimes seen passing through the marine reserve.

Seabirds such as pakahā fluttering shearwaters, kawau tikitiki spotted shags, kāruhiruhi pied shags and tara white-fronted terns are often seen flying over or feeding in the marine reserve. Another rare sighting was a tropical brown booby flying around off the island and landing on the water during April–May 2017.

GETTING THERE

Access to the marine reserve is by private boat, or from the island itself, or from Paraparaumu Beach. Kapiti Island Nature Tours runs a regular ferry service to the island from Paraparaumu Beach, with parking by Paraparaumu Beach and Waikanae Estuary. The nearest train station is Paraparaumu, from where regular buses connect to the beach.

A brown booby was seen at Kapiti Marine Reserve in April 2017.

In winter kekeno New Zealand fur seals haul out at Arapawaiti Point.

Tara white-fronted tern colony on the Waikanae sandspit.

30 WAIKANAE ESTUARY SCIENTIFIC RESERVE

This watery haven by the Waikanae Estuary contains an oasis of brackish lagoons and freshwater lakes next to a sandspit with stunning views of Kapiti Island and inland to the Tararua Range. According to the *eBird NZ* database, over 90 bird species have been recorded here since 1980, making it one of the most bird-diverse wild places in the country.

The Waikanae awa is a taonga with an eclectic diversity of species, among them the ancient scaleless *Galaxias* freshwater fishes, which have a fascinating life cycle. After maturing in the river, they spawn in the intertidal zone and then spend their first six months at sea before returning to swim upriver in spring. The five species here are īnanga, banded kōkopu, kōaro, giant kōkopu and short-jawed kōkopu. The genus name *Galaxias* refers to the constellation of gold, silver and bronze dots and markings on their shiny skin, which resemble a glinting galaxy of stars. They share the awa with tuna short-finned eel and ōrea long-finned eel, as well as tītarakura giant bully, toitoi common bully, panoko torrentfish and piharau lamprey.

Terns are perhaps the most elegant group of seabirds, an observation reflected in their old English name, sea swallows. After a handful of tara white-fronted terns nested on the sandspit here in summer 2021/22, a big nesting colony established the following summer with between one and two thousand adult birds, which raised 140 chicks and presented a fantastic wild spectacle. In late November 2023 a new colony started to establish here. By mid-January 2024 there were about 800 adults and 175 chicks and juveniles.

A total of 11 different tern species have been reported from Waikanae sandspit since 1980, more than at any other site in Aotearoa. In addition, taranui

Tūturiwhatu New Zealand dotterel.

Caspian terns are present year-round, while tarapirohe black-fronted terns are regular visitors in summer and autumn. In summer 2021/22, five other tern species were reported here: Eurasian common, eastern little, white-winged black, sooty and Eurasian black. The discovery of the last species was a first record for Aotearoa. I found a rare Arctic tern with the tara flock here on 28 April 2022, and there are previous records of an Australian gull-billed tern (20 January 2017) and an Australian great crested tern (5 May 1983).

Nothing quite beats a summer walk along this tranquil sandspit to see the graceful flight of the terns as they plunge into the water to catch small fish, or a male bird presenting a female with small fish offerings as part of pair bonding. The best time to visit is in summer from December to February when the tara have their chicks and juveniles.

Tarāpunga red-billed gulls are common around the estuary, and a few tarāpuka black-billed gulls are sometimes seen during autumn and winter, mainly at the south end of Waimanu Lagoon. The endemic tarāpuka is a medium-sized, gleaming white gull with slightly darker grey wings and back than the native tarāpunga, as well as white-tipped black margins to its main flight feathers, black legs and a long, straight black bill. Immature birds have pinkish legs and a dark-tipped pinkish bill.

Pohowera banded dotterels and tōrea pango variable oystercatchers also nest on the sandspit, so watch out for the pohowera running along like little clockwork toys or bobbing up and down while standing on small sandhills or driftwood. Since 2017, tūturiwhatu New Zealand dotterels have bred here. The sand dune area where they nest is usually fenced off, but don't approach them closely if you see them outside the fenced area. Two self-introduced native species originally from Australia – spur-winged plover and black-fronted dotterel – are also present.

Long-distance Arctic migrant wading birds also visit in spring and summer, including kuaka bar-tailed godwits that have flown here from their tundra nesting grounds where they live alongside polar bears and Arctic foxes. After breeding, these imposing, long-billed birds fly across the Pacific Ocean to Aotearoa to escape the Arctic winter. They make the longest non-stop annual migration flight of any non-seabird, taking eight or nine days to fly from Alaska to Aotearoa. During its average 15-year lifespan, a kuaka can fly 385,000 kilometres. Its te reo Māori name comes from its *kua-ka* call.

Ngutu pare wrybill and tōrea South Island pied oystercatchers also stop here on their annual migrations from Te Waipounamu to wintering sites in Te Ika-a-Māui. Ngutu pare is notable as the only bird species in the world with a bill that curves to the right, which it uses to catch insect larvae from under riverbed stones and sift out tiny crustaceans from silt.

Waimanu Lagoon and the nearby freshwater lakes are reliable places to see wetland birds, and the waterfowl flocks here are a winter highlight, including kakīānau black swans, pāteke brown teal and various ducks. Pāpango New Zealand scaup, the endemic black teal with a profile like a toy rubber duck, favours Waimanu Lagoon. Watch for the drake's courtship displays, which involve head-bobbing and head-flicking, and listen for its wobbly *weeee weo-weo weo-weo weo-weoooo* calls as it pursues females.

Kuruwhengi Australasian shoveler drakes have a bluish head and neck with a white crescent on the cheek, and striking

Kāruhiruhi pied shag nest, Waimanu Lagoon breeding colony.

Kuaka bar-tailed godwit pair – the te reo name comes from the *kua-ka* call.

yellow eyes and orange legs. Pārera grey ducks and introduced mallards are also found here. The endemic pārera is a large, darkish brown duck with a grey bill, khaki-olive legs, brown eyes, and body feathers with pale edges. The face is cream-coloured with a dark crown and two dark stripes, and the upper wing is brown with an iridescent green panel. It is easy to confuse with the female mallard, which has orange legs, an orange-and-brown bill, more diffuse eye and bill stripes, a mottled face, and a blue panel on each wing. Hybrids of pārera and mallards are very variable, but often have orange-tinted legs, smudgy head markings and at least some orange on the bill.

The weweia New Zealand dabchick, our small endemic grebe, breeds on the lagoons and lakes usually between August and March. Watch for any fluffy striped juveniles riding on the back of a parental bird, and for the adults' courtship behaviours, which involve the pair swimming around and then at each other.

Kakīānau black swans.

Pārera grey ducks.

If you hear the distinctive *u-tick u-tick* calls of the mātātā fernbird in the raupō habitat by the estuary, wait and you might see one climb up a reed stem to survey its surroundings. There is also a nesting colony of kāruhiruhi pied shags in tall macrocarpa trees by Waimanu Lagoon, where kōtuku ngutupapa royal spoonbills sometimes roost with the shags. Both species feed in the estuary.

There are occasional sightings of the elusive matuku-hūrepo Australasian bittern stalking by the stream that runs through the wetland on the south side of the estuary. From the wooden bridge over the same wetland area, also watch out for the timid koitareke marsh crake. Listen out for its low, muted *brrrrrr* calls. This very small brown rail with black-and-white markings and yellowish legs can sometimes be seen when it comes out to feed on exposed mud as the tide goes out.

The wetlands here attract a colourful variety of attractive dragonflies, such

Male pāpango New Zealand scaup are darker than females and have a distinct golden eye.

Kuruwhengi Australasian shoveler (male) is one of our most colourful duck species.

Koitareke marsh crake is one of the most secretive bird species in Aotearoa.

Pepe ao uri common blue butterfly pair mating.

as the blue-spotted hawker and aurora bluetail, and colourful butterflies such as pepe para riki coastal copper, Māui's copper, pepe ao uri common blue and long-tailed pea blue. Nearby Waikanae Beach has a sparkling diversity of marine shells, including pink sunset shell, small toheroa, tuatua and pipi.

The Department of Conservation (DOC) is working on an ecological restoration project in the Waikanae River catchment, called Waikanae ki Uta ki Tai, which uses a Treaty house partnership model. Ātiawa ki Whakarongotai are the iwi house and DOC, Greater Wellington Regional Council and Kapiti Coast District Council are the kāwanatanga (government) house. The governance group has representatives from iwi and kāwanatanga project partners and also provides governance for a Waikanae Jobs for Nature project, both of which aim to help Ātiawa ki Whakarongotai act as kaitiaki. In November 2020, Waikanae ki Uta ki Tai partners received Jobs for Nature funding for river restoration including native species plantings and pest animal and weed control.

The Waikanae Estuary Care Group has been planting native species and controlling invasive species here for 20 years. Please note that no dogs are allowed on or along the sandspit because it is a breeding site and important habitat for protected threatened bird species. The beach running north from the base of the sandspit is a designated dog-walking area.

Māui's copper butterfly.

GETTING THERE

Trains run from Pōneke to Waikanae station, where the number 280 bus departs from nearby. Once you get off the bus at Barrett Drive next to Waimanu Lagoon, it is a short walk to the estuary and sandspit. Another path runs upstream from the lagoon to a footbridge from where you can walk to the south section of the reserve. Alternatively, from Paraparaumu station the number 262 bus runs along Manly Street. Get off opposite house number 278 near the track entrance to the south end of the reserve. There is parking on Manly Street and Tutere Street.

MORE WILD PLACES

This shortlist of more wild places in Te Upoko-o-te-Ika gives gives a brief summary of their notable features and wildlife. Most are beyond the public transport system, or at its periphery.

Wellington

Mākara Peak – panoramic views, kiwi-nui North Island brown kiwi (seen September 2023), kārearea New Zealand falcon, pīhoihoi New Zealand pipit.

Mākara Beach – coastal birds, kiwi-nui in the hills, tohorā southern right whale, maki orca.

Lower Hutt

Belmont Regional Park (Kelson end) – native forest, kārearea, kākāriki parakeet, mātātā fernbird.

Wainuiomata

Ōrongorongo Track – native forest, ferns, orchids, bush birds.

Baring Head – kekeno New Zealand fur seal, pohowera banded dotterel, cirl bunting, native coastal plants.

Wairarapa

Lake Wairarapa, Domain Reserve to Tauherenīkau delta – tarāpuka black-billed gull, tarapirohe black-fronted tern, taranui Caspian tern, matuku-hūrepo Australasian bittern, migrant waders, wetland habitat.

Lake Wairarapa, Boggy Pond – matuku-hūrepo Australasian bittern, kotoreke marsh crake, pūweto spotless crake, weweia New Zealand dabchick, waterfowl, kōtuku ngutupapa royal spoonbill, taranui, wetland habitat.

Lake Ferry – tarāpuka, tarapirohe, taranui, pohowera, kawau shags, estuary habitat, coastal cobble beach.

Porirua

Rangituhi Colonial Knob – scenic views, native forest, ferns, bush birds including kākāriki.

Porirua Scenic Reserve – mature native forest, ferns, orchids, bush birds including kākāriki.

Kapiti Coast

Queen Elizabeth II Park – wetland habitat with weweia, kāhu swamp harrier, mātātā, waterfowl.

Pharazyn Reserve – large lake, weweia, waterfowl, matuku-hūrepo Australasian bittern, wetland habitat.

Ōtaki Estuary mouth – pohowera, poaka, migrant waders, tarāpuka, tara, taranui, kawau shags, shingle beach, wetland habitat.

Upper Hutt

Silverstream Track – native orchids, ferns, bush birds.

Hutt River, Silverstream to Hutt City – braided river habitat, pūtangitangi paradise shelduck, kererū, kārearea, native bush with big mataī.

Mount Climie – scenic views, native ferns, alpine plants, bush birds.

Fern Gully – native forest, native ferns, native plants, bush birds.

Akatarawa Forest Regional Park – native forest including the largest northern rātā in Aotearoa, native orchids and ferns, koekoeā long-tailed cuckoo, miromiro New Zealand tomtit, pōpokatea whitehead.

Remutaka Trig Track – alpine plants, native orchids, kārearea, koekoeā, kererū New Zealand pigeon.

Remutaka Saddle Track – alpine plants, native orchids (leek, striped sun, *Aporostylis bifolia*), koekoeā, koromako bellbird, kapokapowai New Zealand bush giant dragonfly.

GLOSSARY

Aotearoa The Māori language name for New Zealand.
Awa A river, stream, gully or gorge.
Cryptic Relating to colouration or markings that camouflage a bird or plant in its natural habitat.
Endemic Relating to a species found in a single defined geographical location, such as an island or a country, in this case Aotearoa.
Epiphyte A plant that derives its moisture and nutrients from the air and rain, and usually grows perching on another plant.
Forest & Bird Abbreviated name of the Royal Forest and Bird Protection Society of New Zealand.
Gondwana The large, ancient supercontinent in the southern hemisphere, clustered near the Antarctic Circle, which consisted of the modern-day continents of Antarctica, Zealandia, India, Australia, South America and Africa, before it began to break up about 200 million years ago.
Iwi Tribe; a larger grouping of hapū and whānau units.

Kaitiaki Guardian.
Kaitiakitanga The exercise of guardianship by the tangata whenua of an area in accordance with tikanga Māori in relation to natural and physical resources; includes the ethic of stewardship.
Koru A coil or spiral shape.
Lineage A sequence of species each of which is considered to have evolved from its predecessor.
Mahi Work or effort.
Mana whenua Collective authority over and responsibility for the lands of a descent group; the people who hold this responsibility in an area.
Maunga (mounga in Taranaki dialect) A mountain or peak.
Mauri Life force, the essential quality and vitality of a being or entity. Also used for a physical object, individual, ecosystem or social group in which this essence is located.
Motu Island, or country.
Native species A plant or animal that is indigenous to more than one country.
Ngahere Forest.

Podocarp A tree or shrub with linear or scale-like leaves, which usually has the male and female reproductive organs in separate individuals.

Podocarp forest A type of forest with a mixture of tall podocarps and smaller hardwood trees with an understorey of shrubs, plants and ferns.

Raptor A bird of prey that feeds on live captured prey or carrion.

Relict A population or species that was once more widespread or diverse.

Tamariki Children.

Tangata whenua Indigenous people; Māori.

Taiao The natural environment.

Taonga Treasured things, both physical and intangible.

Te reo Māori The language spoken by the indigenous Māori people of mainland Aotearoa.

Tikanga Processes and behaviours which are correct, just, and appropriate; customs.

Translocation The managed movement of live birds, reptiles, fish, shellfish, insects or plants from one location to another.

Tuna The Māori name for various species of eel.

Vagrant A bird outside its usual breeding and wintering range.

Vegetable sheep A member of *Raoulia*, a genus of endemic cushion plants found only in Aotearoa. Due to their shape and form, they resemble sheep from afar, hence this name.

Wattles Paired fleshy growths hanging from the head or face of a bird.

Whānau Extended family.

Zealandia A long, narrow continent that is now mostly submerged in the South Pacific Ocean.

ACKNOWLEDGEMENTS

I am deeply grateful to publisher Michael Upchurch at Te Papa Press and former publisher Nicola Legat for the opportunity to write and illustrate *Wild Wellington Ngā Taonga Taiao*, to senior project editor Jo Elliott for her diligent work throughout its production, and to Liz Mellish and Rawiri Faulkner for contributing their eloquent texts.

I also want to thank Floor van Lierop for the design, Angela Keoghan for the cover illustration and maps, Jeremy Glyde for the digital imaging, Matt Turner for copyediting the manuscript, Teresa McIntyre and Caren Wilton for the proof reads, and Melissa Bryant for advice and guidance on te reo.

I am also indebted to Te Papa natural history curators and staff for their comments on the manuscript: Carlos Lehnebach, Thom Linley, Felix Marx, Heidi Meudt, Colin Miskelly, Leon Perrie, Phil Sirvid, Lara Shepherd, Andrew Stewart, Alan Tennyson and Kerry Walton. Likewise, Nikki McArthur and Tim Park for their invaluable comments. If any errors of fact have crept into the text, they are my responsibility.

No book could be written and illustrated without the help of many others, so I also want to thank the following for their invaluable help with research and/or field work: Sally Bain, Dallas Bishop, Melissa Boardman, Roger Brent Smith, Scott Brooks, Andrew Broome, Mike and Jane Camm, Geoff de Lisle, Jonathan Delich, Israel Didham, Joe Dillon, Helen Duncan, Oskar Ehrhardt, Sally Eyre, Johannes Fischer, Robbie Graham, George Gibbs, Reino Grundling, Cliff Keilty, Shirley Kerr, Peter Langlands, Vladimir Macoviciuc, Sarah Milicich, Rod Morris, Lee Ormsby Andricksen, Vandy Pollard, Ray Smith, Christopher Stephens, David Thomas, Oscar Thomas, John van den Hoeven, Hilton and Melva Ward, Zac Warren, Imogen Warren, Steve Wass, Duncan Watson, Steve Wood, Andreas Zeller, and the late Wade Doak, Roger Grace and Geoff Park.

I would also like to thank my partner Stephanie Mills and our children Marika, Louis and Istvan for their comments and support.

During the writing I found Te Papa's Te Taiao Nature Series on the native birds, plants, insects, and shells of Aotearoa, and the *New Zealand Birds Online* digital encyclopaedia to be important reference resources, so would also like to thank their various authors.

Michael Szabo, Island Bay

To conclude this traverse of wild Wellington I wish to acknowledge the team who have worked together to share their knowledge of this place we call home and know intimately: Vicki Hollywell, who kept us on task, writer historians Richard Te One and Matiu Jennings, Neavin Broughton, who provided the cultural support we always need, and Coral McLennan, a great researcher for photos and digital media. Finally, my thanks go to the ahu whenua trust who support the cultural narrative by holding the history records and having the courage to lodge our treaty claim, and continue to advocate strongly in all forums for our voices to reach the spirit world.

Liz Mellish MNZM, Amokura, Te Wharewaka o Pōneke

Te Papa Press wishes to acknowledge and thank Liz Mellish and her team, and Rawiri Faulkner, Raylene Bishop and Jasmine Arthur for their support of this book and sharing their mātauranga. Thanks also to Lee-Anne Duncan and *NZ Life & Leisure* magazine for allowing us to adapt the story on page 215–217.

We are grateful for generous funding from the Te Papa Foundation, which has enabled us to send a copy to each school in Te Upoko-o-te-Ika, and to the Deane Endowment Trust for their continued support.

ABOUT THE AUTHOR AND PHOTOGRAPHER

Michael Szabo is the author of *Native Birds of Aotearoa* (Te Papa Press 2022) and the editor of *Birds New Zealand* magazine. He was principal author of *Wild Encounters: A Forest & Bird Guide to Discovering New Zealand's Unique Wildlife* (Penguin 2009) and one of the principal authors of *New Zealand Birds Online*. A former editor of *Forest & Bird* magazine, he has also written about natural history and conservation for *New Scientist, New Zealand Geographic, Wilderness*, and the *Sunday Star-Times*.

He has worked in senior roles for several conservation and environmental organisations, as campaigns manager at Greenpeace Aotearoa, communications manager at BirdLife International, communications manager at Forest & Bird, and as the founding director of the Pew Charitable Trust's Kermadecs Ocean Sanctuary Project. He also wrote *Making Waves I & II* (Reed Books 1990; Greenpeace Aotearoa 2021), which chart the history of Greenpeace's campaigns in Aotearoa, the South Pacific and Antarctica from 1972 to 2020.

His photography has also been published in *Forest & Bird, Birds New Zealand, Wilderness, New Zealand Geographic* and *Greenpeace Aotearoa* magazines.

IMAGE CREDITS

All photographs are copyright © Michael Szabo, except pages:

8, **17** by Yoan Jolly © Museum of New Zealand Te Papa Tongarewa, with thanks to model, Elena Lee;
23 William Trethewey sculpture of Kupe, Hine-te-aparangi and Pekahourangi © Neil Price;
29 kiwi pukupuku little spotted kiwi © Leon Berard;
40 mouku hen and chickens fern © Leon Perrie;
50 titiwai glowworms © Dougal Townsend;
56 pānoko thread fern © Leon Perrie;
57 petako sickle spleenwort © Leon Perrie;
58 view from Mount Tarikākā © Mel Durling;
64 Pōneke Wellington waterfront by Kate Whitley © Museum of New Zealand Te Papa Tongarewa;
71 view of Bush City by Michael Hall © Museum of New Zealand Te Papa Tongarewa;
82 fly agaric toadstool *iNaturalist*/Jon Sullivan, CC-BY 4.0;
87 Oruaiti Pā site by Neil Price © Wellington City Council;
88 looking over to South Island © Katie/Flickr;
91 mangō taniwha great white shark © Kina Scollay;
160 ornate skink by Anthony Whitaker. Museum of New Zealand Te Papa Tongarewa, gift of Vivienne Whitaker, 2020, CT.068264;
189 matuku-hūrepo Australasian bittern © Bradley Shields;
200 Percy Scenic Reserve © David Goldthorpe;
221 spur-winged plover © Phil Battley;
232 rowi Ōkarito brown kiwi © Leon Berard;
239 koekoeā long-tailed cuckoo © Tony Stoddard;
253 Māui's copper butterfly © Saryu Mae.

Te Papa Press is grateful for the support of the photographers and copyright holders who have contributed to this book.

INDEX

Bold page numbers also indicate images.

āhuruhuru 243
aihe 9, 10, 22, 65, 86, 91, 100, 102, **103**, 124, 128, 129, 138, 156, 159, 228, 243, **244**
akakaiore 39, 48, **49**, 201
Akatarawa Forest Regional Park 255
Akatarewa Pā 23
akatawhiwhi 63, 151, 195, 209
akeake 74
albatrosses 9, 10, 93, 102, 129, **132**, 133, 138, 139: Antipodean albatross 129, 133; black-browed albatross 129, **130**, 133, **135**, 139; Buller's albatross 129, 134, **135**, **136**; light-mantled sooty albatross 129, **130**; northern royal albatross 129, **130**, 131, 133, **134**; Salvin's albatross 129, **130**, 133; shy albatross 133; southern royal albatross 129, **130**, 131, 133, **136**, wandering albatross 129, 131; white-capped albatross 129, 133, **135**
alpine plants 15, 35, 110, 200–1, 203: collection 15, 145, 200–5
anemones, sea 243
angiangi 193, **195**
araara 103
Arapawaiti Point 243, 244, **245**
Atatürk Memorial 97
Ātiawa ki Whakarongotai 253
aua 65

bachelor's button 119
Baring Head 145, 254
Barking Emu Track 110
beaked whale:
 Arnoux's beaked whale 106, 228;
 Shepherd's beaked whale 127, 228
Beech Track 27, 31, 32

beeches: red beech 10, 32, **164**, 168, 171, 172, **175**, 176–8, 181, 182, 184, 193, **197**; southern beeches *Nothofagus* 193: goblin forest 10, 193, 195, **197**
bees, native **74**, 76
beetles 210: longhorn beetle 76; New Zealand reticulated stag beetle 205; New Zealand striped longhorn beetle 184; stinking ground beetle 241; tiger beetle 166, 168, 184, **185**
bellbird 11, 25, 32, 36, 41, 45, 48, 63, 95, **150**, 166, 177, 181, 197, 201, 211, 233
Belmont Regional Park 143, 146–51, 254: Kelson end 254
bidibid **95**, 97
bindweed: New Zealand bindweed 103, 156; shore bindweed 97, 188
Birds New Zealand 133, 139, 219, 234
bittern, Australasian 188, **189**, 250, 254, 255
blennies 105
Blossom (ihupuku southern elephant seal) 68
bluebell, Cook Strait coastal 114, **118**, 119
blueberry, New Zealand 171, 178, 207
booby, brown 244, **245**
Breaker Bay 56, 90–3, 94, 95, 97
Brooklyn wind turbine 79, 110
broom: native broom 31, **33**, 35, 205, 207; stout dwarf broom *Carmichaelia monroi* **205**
bullies: blue-gilled bully 39, 151, 211; common bully 31, 166, 187, 191, 199, 247; giant bully 187, 247; red-finned bully 151, 180
Burdan's Gate, Eastbourne 187, 191
Bush City exhibition (Te Papa) 68, **71**
buttercups: alpine buttercup 203; sand buttercup 123, 188;

scree buttercup 203; swamp buttercup 187
butterfish 99
butterflies 9, 12, 107, 151, 188: common blue butterfly 123, **252**, 253; copper butterfly 56, **107**, 110, **111**, 121, 123, 151, 162, 241, 253; forest glade butterfly 105; forest ringlet butterfly 166, **167**, 197; long-tailed pea blue butterfly 253; Māui's copper butterfly 56, 63, 162, **253**; monarch butterfly 51, 56, **61**, 63; North Island coastal copper butterfly 63, 107, 121, 151, 162, 241, 253; North Island glade copper butterfly 56, **57**, 63, 83; painted lady butterfly 63; red admiral butterfly 36, 63, **74**, 76, 83, 110, **113**, 121, 123, 151, 162, 166, 168, 184, 197, 241; yellow admiral butterfly 36, 42, 56, **61**, 63, 76, 83, 121, 123, 162, 166, 168, 197, 205
Butterfly Creek 145, 166-7, 176–85, 187

cabbage tree **13**, 42, 60, 68, 74, 99
Capital Kiwi Project 14, 109, 110
Chaffers Marina 65, 68, 71
cicadas 51, 76, 99, **118**, 119, 121, 124, 151, 162, 166, 188, 207: April green cicada 151; chirping cicada **118**, 119, 121; chorus cicada 76, **208**; clapping cicada 162; lesser bronze cicada 151
cirl bunting 93, 254
clematis: Forster's clematis 113, **181**; leafless clematis 124; native clematis 68, **70**, 151, 181, 209
Clinical Track 79
clubmoss 48
cod: bearded rock cod 243; blue cod 99, **101**, 242
conservation 12-15: groups and organisations 13–15;

262

Conservation Volunteers New Zealand 191
Cook Canyon 9, 132–9
coprosma shrubs 63, **147**
coral, black 243
cottonwood 63, 99, 123
crab, purple rock 100, **101**
crake: marsh crake 250, **252**, 254; spotless crake 187, 222, **223**, 254
cranesbill, alpine 110
crayfish, freshwater 63, 166, 187, 211
crustaceans 99, 248
cuckoos: long-tailed cuckoo 11, 161, 166, 168, 180, 197, 211, 237, **239**, 255; shining cuckoo 36, 39, **57**, 63, 76, 79, 95, 150, 166, 168, 180, 182, 197, 207, 237
cushion plants 10, 188, 203

dabchick, New Zealand **187**, 250, 254, 255
daisies, tree 201: coastal tree daisy 114, 123; Gardner's tree daisy 201; heketara tree daisy 201; Kirk's tree daisy 39; rangiora tree daisy 60, 74, 81, 176, 201
daisies: bachelor's button 119; black scree button daisy 203; *Celmisia* 'mangaweka'; mat daisy 114, 123, **190**; mountain daisy *Brachyglottis lagopus* 119, **120**; papatāniwhaniwha 119; *Raoulia glabra* 114; *Raoulia hookerii* 123
damselflies 166: aurora bluetail 253; blue damselfly 35, 184, **185**; red damselfly **183**, 184, 222
daphne, New Zealand 119, 188, **190**
Department of Conservation (DOC) 14, 15, 100, 110, 144, 161, 162, 186, 191, 199, 203, 214, 216, 218, 228, 231, 234–5, 241, 253
dolphins 16, 129: common dolphin 9, 10, 22, 65, 86, 91, 100, 102, **103**, 124, 128, 129, 138, 156, 159, 228, 243, **244**; dusky dolphin 138; Hector's dolphin 156, 244
dotterels 16: banded dotterel 145, 167, 184, 188, **190**, 191, 219, 221, 248, 254, 255; black-fronted dotterel 248; New Zealand dotterel 221, **247**, 248
Dracophyllum **115**, 203

dragonflies 184, 250: blue-spotted hawker 184, 188, 222, **223**, 253; dusk dragonfly 184; Gray's dragonfly 188; New Zealand bush giant dragonfly 11, 42, 56, **62**, 63, 76, 114, 119, 166, 184, 188, 197, 211, 218; ranger dragonfly 184, 188, 222, **223**
drummer, silver 243
ducks: grey duck 187, **250**; mallard 250
dunes 16, 86, 95, 97, **100**, 103, 105, 156, **157**, 248

East Harbour Regional Park (EHRP) 10, 144, 164–85, 186, 209
eBird NZ 12, 246
eels 21, 39, 142, 145, 187: conger eel 144; long-finned eel 39, 151, 166, 187, 199, 211, 247; short-finned eel 39, 151, 166, 187, 199, 211, 247
extinct species 13, 27, 28, 31, 41, 53, 58, 105, 193, 237: huia 13, 27, 41, 53, 193, 237
eyebright, North Island 110, **114**

Facebook groups 12, 68, 107, 139
falcon, New Zealand 9, 11, 13, 16, 25, 28, 30, 31, 36, 39, 48, 55, 59, 72, **73**, 74, **75**, 79, 95, 102, 110, 123, 144, 147, 150, 166, 168, 177, 181–2, 197, 211, 233, 237, 239, 254, 255
fantail, New Zealand 39, 41, 55, 63, 68, 76, 93, **149**, 150, 161, 166, 168, 181, 211
Fern Gully 255
fernbird 11, 222, **223**, 233, 250, 254, 255
ferns, filmy 6, **47**, 172: drooping filmy fern 41, 46, **47**, 195; fan-like filmy fern 184, 195, 209; hairy filmy fern 209; rusty filmy fern 209, **211**
ferns, fork 46, **47**, 166, 178, **207**: drooping fork fern *Tmesipteris elongata* 48
ferns, ground 10, 35, 39, 42, 254, 255: bristle fern 60; bristly cloak fern 114; butterfly fern **32**, 60, 114; button fern 178; carrier tangle fern 209; crepe fern 41; crown fern **195**; Cunningham's maidenhair fern 119, 178, **179**, 203; fine-leaved parsley fern 110; fragrant fern 46, 178, **179**; gully fern 81, 119, **151**, 241; hen and chickens fern 32, **40**, 41, 178; hound's tongue fern 56, **57**, 74, 172, 178, 203, 241; kidney fern 60, 151, 172, **175**, 178, 184, 195; lace fern 60; lance fern 46, **47**, 119, 151, 195; maidenhair fern 46, 178; rasp fern 76; ring fern 110, **112**, 184; rock fern 114, 124; screw fern 172, 178; shaking brake 114; stalked adder's tongue fern 42, 203, **204**; sweet fern 32, **33**, 60; tangle fern **208**, 209; thread fern **56**; umbrella fern 178, 209; water fern 195
ferns, hard: alpine hard fern 110, **112**; mountain hard fern 110, **112**; shore 119, **120**
ferns, kiokio palm-leaf 195: small kiokio palm-leaf fern 114, 178, 195, **196**; swamp kiokio palm-leaf fern 119
ferns, shield: blue shield fern 76; climbing shield fern 203
ferns, spleenwort 48, 110
ferns, tree 9, 36, 48, 166, 255: black tree fern 32, 41, 81, 151, 172, **175**, 184, 201, 209, 241; golden tree fern 209; silver fern 32, 41, **46**, 53, **54**, 60, 81, 151, 172, 178, 184, 209; slender tree fern 151, 195, 241; Smith's tree fern 151; soft tree fern 172, 195, 209, 241
fish, freshwater 10, 31, 39, 63, 142, 143, 151, 166, 180, 187, 191, 199, 211, 247
five-finger 31, 53,181, 240
flax linen, native 36, 119
flax: coastal flax **14**, 25, **94**, 95, 99, 103, 105, 114, 123, 156, 234; New Zealand flax 143
flounder, sand 103, 144
Forest & Bird 99, 161, 162, 256: Places for Penguins project 14, 100; reserve 218, 234
forget-me-nots 203: cushion 203; *Myosotis exinia* **204**
Friends of Baring Head 191
Friends of Mana Island (FOMI) 14, 223–4
Friends of Otari–Wilton's Bush Trust 14, 43
Friends of Taputeranga Marine Reserve 100

frog, Maud Island 11, 31
fuchsia: fuchsia hybrid, *F. excorticata* x *F. perscandens* 119; New Zealand creeping fuchsia **35**, 201; tree fuchsia 25, **35**, 60, 68
fulmar, Antarctic 133, **137**
fungi 42, 43, 166, 183: anemone stinkhorn fungus 77, 151, 167, 178, 184; *Armillaria* mushrooms **51**, 183; austral honey mushroom 56, 63; blackening waxcap 184; blue-green potato fungus 178; chanterelle mushroom *Cantharellus wellingtonensis* 51; collared earthstar **48**, 51, 63, 77; coral fungi (*Clavaria* species) 42, 151, 167, 178, 184, 205; *Entoloma canoconicum* 151; *Entoloma hochstetteri* 167, 178; green verdigris waxcap 151, 167, 178, **179**; jewelled amanita mushroom 56; lemon honeycap mushroom *Armillaria limonea* 42, 178, **179**, 184; lilac coral fungus 151, 184, 205; mycorrhizal fungi 166, 178; native shiitake mushroom 178; orange waxgill mushroom 42, 151; pink gill mushroom 184; red-capped fly agaric toadstool 51, 56, 77, **82**, 83; red coral fungus 178; ruby bonnet 51, **82**, 83; sandy stiltball mushroom **76**, 77; southern beech amanita mushroom 184; southern false morel mushroom 178, 184; straw flycap mushroom 178; velvet earthstar 178; violet potato fungus 178, 184; waxgills 63; white basket fungus 63, 77, **82**, 83, 205

Galaxias freshwater fishes 199, 247: dwarf galaxias 199, 211
gannet, Australasian 65, 93, 102, **138**, 139, 155, 159, **160**, 227
geckos 9, 42, 81, 62, 217, 241: barking gecko 162, **163**, **196**, 199, 233, 241; goldstripe gecko 11, 233, 241; minimac gecko 123, **124**, mokopirirakau form of ngahere gecko 199, 241; ngahere gecko 42, **43**, 82, 162, 233, **240**; Raukawa gecko 97, 162, 166, 199, **232**, 233, 241; Tohu's gecko 233

gentians 203: tall gentian 203
George Denton Park 78, 79, 81
glowworm **50**, 51, 68
goatfish 243
goblin forest 10, 193, 195, **197**
godwit, bar-tailed 153, 219, 227, 248, **249**
golden scabweed *Raoulia australis* 114
Gollans Stream 180, 181, 184, 187
Gondwana 11, 27, 193, 256
grass, Cook's scurvy 156, 234
grasshopper **170**
grass-tree, needle-leaf 10, 114, **115**
Greater Wellington Regional Council (GWRC) 14, 31, 53, 100, 167, 191, 193, 197, 199, 207, 253
grey warbler 39, 41, 63, 93, 110, 150, 161, 166, 168, **169**, 181, 184, 211
groundsel, guano 156
grouper 133
gulls 11, 16, 159, 227: black-billed gull 153, **155**, 248, 254; red-billed gull 93, **102**, 105, 107, 127, 131, **152**, 153, 225, 233, 248; southern black-backed gull 102, 107, 127, 225, **227**
Gunnera hamiltonii 203, **204**
gurnard 144

haku 99, 103, 243
hangehange 81, 177, 181
hāpuku 133
harakeke 143
harebells, rock 36, 110, 178, 180; violet rock harebell **109**, 110, 178; *Wahlenbergia matthewsii* 178, 180; *W. pygmaea* 110; *W. violacea* **109**, 110, 178
harore 42, 178, **179**, 184
harrier, swamp 59, 110, 123, 168, 182, 219, **220**, 221–2, 237, 255
Hawkins Hill **108**, 110, 113, **115**
heketara 201
Hem of Remutaka 191
here rō 56, 82, 162, 205
herons 221: reef heron 95, **96**, 102, 105, 127, 153, 225, 227; white heron **153**; white-faced heron 102, **104**, 105, 127, 153, 188, 218, 219, 221, 225

heruheru 41
hihi 9, 11, 13, 25, **26**, 32, 79, 199, 237, **238**, 240
hīnau 25, 41, 42, 46, 53, 151, 171, 177, 181, 192, 206, 207
hoki 89, 129
Hole-in-the-Wall Bay 243
horokaka 95, 123, 188, **190**
Houghton Bay 103, **104**, 105, 107
hoverflies 76
huhu 76
huia 13, 27, 41, 53, 193, 237
huku 51, 56, **61**, 63
hūperei 81, 165, 171, **173**, 177, 178, **182**, 183, 195, 241
huruhuru tapairu 178
huruhuru whenua 241
Hutt City Council 14, 201, 203
Hutt River 145, 152, 155, 156, 201, **206**, 207, 255: mouth 142, 143, 152–7: Silverstream to Hutt City 255

ice plant, New Zealand 95, **107**, 123, 188, **190**
ihupuku 68, **70**, 103, 161
īnanga (fish) 39, 180, 247
īnanga (needle-leaf grass-tree) 10, 114, **115**
iNaturalist NZ 12, 100, 166
irirangi 41, 46, **47**, 195
iris, Edgar's mīkoikoi 167, 178
Island Bay 14, 68, 100, **104**, 105, **106**: sand dunes **100**, 105

jasmine, New Zealand **40**, 41, 181

kahawai 99, 142, 144
kahikatea **36**, **37**, 142, 178, 181, 195, 206
kāhu 59, 110, 123, 168, 182, 219, **220**, 221–2, 237, 255
kahukōwhai 36, 42, 56, **61**, 63, 76, 83, 121, 123, 162, 166, 168, 197, 205
kahukura 36, 63, **74**, 76, 83, 110, **113**, 121, 123, 151, 162, 166, 168, 184, 197, 241
kaihua **40**, 41, 181
kaikōmako, Three Kings 201
Kaikōura Ranges 58, **88**, 97, 99, 108, 122, 145

Kaitoke Regional Park swingbridge track circuit 145, **206**, 206–11
Kaiwharawhara Stream 21, 35, 36: valley **34**
kākā 9, 10, 11, 13, 16, 21, 25, 28, 36, **40**, 41–2, 45, 48, 55, 59, 73, 76, 79, 95, 110, 199, 217, 240
kākahi 31, 187, 191
kākāpō 13, 42, 188, 193, **198**, 199
kākāriki 42: red-crowned kākāriki 11, 13, 25, 41, 42, 48, 55, 63, 79, 93, 144, 146, **147**, 158, 161, 168, 182, 199, 240, 254; yellow-crowned kākāriki 146, **147**, 197, 233
kakiānau 153, 187, 248
kama 195
kāmahi 164, 171, 181, 206, 211
kanono 81
kānuka 240
Kapiti Coast 9, 127, 215, 236–45, 255
Kapiti Coast District Council 14, 253
Kapiti Island 214, 215–17, 225, **236**, 237, **242**, 246
Kapiti Island Nature Reserve 10, 11, 13, 15, 27, 28, 139, 144, 225, 236–41
Kapiti Island Nature Tours 215–17, 237, 241, 244
Kapiti Island Strategic Advisory Committee 241
Kapiti Marine Reserve 15, 16, **242**, 242–5
kapokopowai 11, 42, 56, **62**, 63, 76, 114, 119, 166, 184, 188, 197, 211, 218
karaka 41, 46, 74, 201
kareao 39, 142, 209
kārearea 9, 11, 13, 16, 25, 28, 30, 31, 36, 39, 48, 55, 59, 72, **73**, 74, **75**, 79, 95, 102, 110, 123, 144, 147, 150, 166, 168, 177, 181–2, 197, 211, 233, 237, 239, 254, 255
karetai hurukoko 131, **133**, **136**, 139
karetai kauae mā **131**, 134
Karori 9, 24: lighthouse 127
Karori Sanctuary Trust 32
karoro 102, 107, 127, 225, **227**
kāruhiruhi 32, 225, 227, **229**, 233, 244, **249**, 250
karuwhai 203
kātote 151, 172, 195, 209, 241
katydids: blackish meadow katydid 241; common katydid 121

kauri 39, 42
kawakawa 53, **54**, 81, 151, 166
kawau tikitiki 11, **92**, 93, 162, 244
kawau tūī 187, **226**, 227
kawaupaka 187, **226**, 227
kekeno 9, 10, 65, 91, 94, **97**, 100, 102, **104**, 105, 109, 122, **126**, 129, 155, 161, 228, 243, 244, **245**, 254, **255**
kēkēwai 35, 184, **185**
kelp, bull 91, **92**, 99, 124, 243
kererū 25, **40**, 41, 73, **76**, 93, 110, 147, 166, 215, 255
Kererū Track 168–76
kiekie 41, 151, 178, 181, **185**, 201, 209
kihikihi 99, 119, 124, 151, 166, 188
kihikihi wawā 51, 76, **118**, 119, 162, 166, **208**
kihitara **183**, 184, 222
kiki pounamu 121
Kilbirnie 14, 87
kingfish, yellowtail 99, 103, 144, 243
kingfisher, sacred 35, 48, 55, 76, 95, **96**, 151, 161, 166, **188**, 219
kiokio palm-leaf ferns 195: small kiokio palm-leaf fern 114, 178, 195, **196**; swamp kiokio palm-leaf fern 119
kiwakiwa 195
kiwi 9, 10, 11, 13, 14, 21, 110, 217: little spotted kiwi 11, 13, 25, 27, **29**, 79, 199, 217, 237; North Island brown kiwi 11, 14, 109, 193, **196**, 197, 254; Ōkarito brown kiwi 11, 199, 231, **232**, 233
kiwi pukupuku 11, 13, 25, 27–8, **29**, 79, 199, 217, 237
kiwi-nui 11, 14, 109, 193, **196**, 197, 254
Kōanga (Spring) (rāpoka leopard seal) 68
kōaro 39, 63, 199, 211, 247
koekoeā 11, 161, 166, 168, 180, 197, 211, 237, **239**, 255
kohekohe 10, 35, 39, 41, **44**, **45**, 46, 48, 53, 60, 99, 119, 151, 201, 234, **237**, 240
kohukohu, perching 201
kohurangi 39
koinga 10, 68, **70**, 71, 228
koitareke 250, **252**
kōkako 9, 10, 11, 13, 199, 216, **237**, 239

kōkopu 143: banded kōkopu 31, 39, 63, 166, 180, 187, 247; giant kōkopu 39, 166, 180, 187, 199, 247; short-jawed kōkopu 39, 199, 247
kōkōwai 31, **161**, 162, 233
kōnini **35**, 201
korimako 11, 25, 32, 36, 41, 45, 48, 63, 95, **150**, 166, 177, 181, 197, 201, 211, 233
Korimako Track 168–75
Korohiwa Track 180–4
korokio 110, **112**
Korokoro Dam Loop Track 143, **146**, 146–51
Korokoro Stream 143, 151
koromiko hebe **74**, 76, **80**, 110, **111**, 113, 119, 123, 162: *Veronica parviflora* 113; Waitākere rock koromiko 201
kororā 9, 11, 14, 22, **65**, **69**, 93, 95, 99, 105, 139, 144, 159, 167, 217, 233, 237, 243
kōtare 35, 48, 55, 76, 95, **96**, 151, 161, 166, **188**, 219
kōtuku **153**
kōtuku ngutupapa **92**, 93, 153, 219, 227, 240, 250, 254
kōtukutuku 25, **35**, 60, 68
kōura (freshwater crayfish) 63, 166, 187, 211; (rock lobster) 99, **101**, 103, 105, 242, 243
kōwaowao 241
kōwhai 10, 31, 36, 39, 45, 201: Cook Strait kōwhai 144; small-leaved kōwhai 144
Kōwhai Track 166, 176, 177, 180–4
kōwhangatara 97, 105, 156, 188
kuaka (bar-tailed godwit) 153, 219, 227, 248, **249**
kuaka (common diving petrel) 11, 134, 162, **231**
kuruwhengi 187, 240, 248, 250, **251**
kuta 187

ladybird, steel-blue 184
lake clubrush 187
Lake Ferry 97, 254
Lake Kōhangapiripiri 31, **186**, 187, 191
Lake Kōhangaterā 186–91
Lake Ōnoke 97
Lake Wairarapa: Boggy Pond 254;

Domain Reserve to Tauherenīkau delta 254
lamprey 199, 247
lawyer: bush lawyer 41, **60**, 63, 113; swamp lawyer 195
leatherjacket, velvet 105
lemonwood 53, **54**, 207, 209
Leptinella squalida 119
lichens 193, **195**
lilies, perching 39, 181, 195, 197, **209**
lobelia, shore 95
lobster, rock 99, **101**, 103, 105, 242, 243
locust, migratory 114
Lower Hutt 139, 146, 152, 205, 254
Lyall Bay 14, 103

māakoako 103, 222
Mackenzie Track 176–80
mackerel, jack 103
macrocarpa 53, 77, 250
māhoe 25, 53, 60, 74, 81, 114, 123, 176, 181, 201, 234, 240: Cook Strait māhoe 105, 114; thick-leaved māhoe 97
māikaika **170**, 171, 172, 177, 183
maikaika 56, 63, 81, 119, 151, 172, **176**, 177
maikuku 48, 56, 63, 119, 151, 171, 172, **173**, 177, 178, 183–4, 241
Mainland Island Restoration Operation (MIRO) 14, 167, 191
maire, black 46, **46**, 206
mākaka (broom) 31, **33**, 35, 201, 203, 205, 207
mākaka (saltmarsh ribbonwood) 95
Mākara 39, 53, 109, 127, **234**
Mākara Beach 254
Mākara Peak 254
Mākaro Ward Island 143
maki 9, 10, 22, 65, 66, **67**, 71, 91, 98, 100, 102, 105–6, 124, 129, **132**, 133, 156, 159, 176, 219, 228, 244, 254
makomako **59**, 60
mamaku 32, 41, 81, 151, 172, **175**, 184, 201, 209, 241
Mana Island Scientific Reserve 11, 14, 28, 127, 139, 147, 224, 225, **230**, 230–4, **234**, 235
manaia 9, 98, **99**, 100, 103, 105
mangō taniwha **91**

mantis, New Zealand 121, 162, **163**
mānuka **74**, 164, 176, 177, 180
māpou 74, 201
māpunga 187–8, **189**
mararī 99
marguerites, snow 203
Marine Education Centre, Island Bay **104**, 105, 106
marine reserves 10, 12, 15, 16: Kapiti Marine Reserve 15, 242–5; Taputeranga Marine Reserve 10, 15, 87, 98–107; visitor rules 16
matai 35, 36, 181, **194**, 195, 197, 240, 255
Matairangi Mount Victoria 14, 23, 71, **72**, 72–7, 144
Matariki (tohorā southern right whale) 66, 103, 156
mātātā (fernbird) 11, 222, **223**, 233, 250, 254, 255
mātātā (lace fern) 60
Matiu Somes Island 11, 14, 15, 131, 139, 143–4, **158**: scientific and historic reserve 147, 158–63, 240
Matiu Somes Island Charitable Trust 14, 161–2
Matiu Somes Island Kaitiaki Board 159, 161, 162
matua mauku 46, **47**, 172
matuku moana 95, **96**, 102, 105, 127, 153, 225, 227
matuku-hūrepo 188, **189**, 250, 254, 255
māwhitiwhiti 114
Me Heke Ki Pōneke *see* Wellington City Council
mega-dolphins *see* maki orca
mīkoikoi 167, 178
mingimingi 123, 177: dwarf 110
Miramar Peninsula 14, 86, 94, 153, 156
MIRO (Mainland Island Restoration Operation) 14, 167, 191
miro 35, 39, 41, 181, 206, 240
miromiro **149**, 150, 168, 177, 182, 193, 197, 207, 255
mirror bush 74, 103
mistletoe, red 178, **180**, 209
Moa Point 89
mohimohi 65
moho pererū **220**, 222
mōkarakara **111**, 114, **157**

moki: blue moki 91, 99; red moki **243**
mokimoki 46, 178, **179**
Moko (rimu) 21, **38**, 39, 41, 42
moko kākāriki 162, **163**, **196**, 199, 233, 241
moko mangaeka 11, 233, 241
moko pāpā 97, 162, 166, 199, **232**, 233, 241
mokomoko 82, **97**, 123, 124, 151, 166, 177, 233, **234**, 241
Mokopuna Island 143, 162
morepork 25, **30**, 31, 55, 63, 74, 79, 95, 166, 217, 233, 237, **260**
mosses 184, 193, 195: giant moss *Dawsonia superba* 195; umbrella moss 184
moths: brown forest flash 197; *Chersadaula ochrogastra* 56; geometrid day moth 119; green carpet owlet moth 197; kāmahi green spindle moth 211; magpie moth **111**, 114, **157**; māhoe moth 56; *Orocrambus fugitivellus* 119; pūriri moth 56, 211, 241
Motu Kairangi Miramar Peninsula 14, 86, 94, 153, 156
mouku 32, **40**, 41, 178
Mount Climie 255
Mount Tarikākā 53, **58**, 58–63
mountain toropapa 195
Mt Vic Revegers 74
Mt Victoria Bush Regeneration Group 74
Mt Victoria Vermin Trappers 74
muehlenbeckia **80**
mullet 142, 144: yelloweye mullet 65
Muritai Eastbourne 14, 145, 164–7, 176
Muritai Track 176–80
mussels: freshwater mussels 31, 187, 191; horse mussel 184

nau 156, 234
nettle, stinging 63, 119, **120**
New Zealand Birders Facebook group 12, 139
New Zealand Native Orchids Facebook group 12
ngahere (gecko) 42, **43**, 82, 162, 199, 211, 233, **240**, 241,
ngaio 53, 81, 114, 201, **204**

Ngā Kaimanaaki o Te Waimapihi, Polhill Protectors 79, 81
Ngake 23, 87
ngāokeoke 63
Ngāti Toa Rangatira 14, 100, 110, 214, 234, 241
ngutu pare 248
nīkau 142, **148**, 151, 177, 178, 181, 201, 239
nudibranchs 105, 127

octopus 88, 99, 100, 103, **104**, 105, 243: blanket octopus 243; paper nautilus 243
ongaonga 63, 119, **120**
orange roughy 129
orca 9, 10, 22, 65, 66, **67**, 71, 91, 98, 100, 102, 105–6, 124, 129, **132**, 133, 156, 159, 176, 219, 228, 244, 254
orchids 9, 10, 17, 32, 38, 164, 165, 166, 171–2, 177, 195, 209: *Aporostylis bifolia* 255; bamboo orchid 39, 48, **49**, 63, 165, 172, 178, 195; big red spider orchid 183; black orchid 81, 165, 171, **173**, 177, 178, **182**, 183, 195, 241; *Caladenia* orchids 165, 171, 172, **173**, 177, 209; *Caladenia bartlettii* 171; *Caladenia chlorostyla* 171, 172, **173**, 177; *Caladenia chlorostyla* 'green fingers' **173**; *Caladenia chlorostyla* 'minor' 177; *Caladenia lyallii* 209; *Caladenia variegata* 171, **173**, 177; Christmas orchid 165; common onion orchid 56, 63, 81, 119, 151, 172, **176**, 177; common sun orchid 48, 56, 63, 119, 151, 171, 172, **173**, 177, 178, 183–4, 241; *Corybas hatchii* 209; *Corybas iridescens* 183; *Corybas macranthus* **174**, 183, 184; *Corybas oblongus* 209; *Corybas rivularis* 'whiskers' 209; *Corybas trilobus* 56, 171, 172, 178, 183, 184; *Corybas trilobus* 'remutaka' 171, 172, **174**; *Corybas vitreus* 56; Easter orchid 56, 151, 172, **174**, 177–8, 183; fleshy green tree orchid 172, 177; flowering spider orchid 171; gnat orchid 178, **182**, 183–4; grass-leaved greenhood orchid 172, 177, 183; green bird orchid 56, **57**, 63, 151, 177; green fleshy tree orchid 172; greenhood orchid 32, 48, **49**, 56, 81, 119, 151, 165, 172, **174**, **175**, 177, **182**, 183, 184, 241; Hatch's sun orchid 171, **173**, 177; horned orchid 172, **174**; ladies' tresses orchid 203, **204**; leek orchid 63, 255; mountain caps orchid 209; New Zealand mountain greenhood orchid 63; onion orchids 56, 63, 81, 119, 151, 165, 172, **176**, 177; pixie cap orchid 172, 177, 178, **179**, 183–4, 241; *Pterostylis australis* 172, 184; *Pterostylis banksii* 172; *Pterostylis cardiostigma* 172, 177, 184; *Pterostylis montana* 172; pygmy tree orchid 119, **120**, 172, 183; silver-back spider orchid 119, **174**, 183; slender greenhood orchid 114; slender sun orchid 171, 178; small onion orchid 63; spider orchids 56, 119, 165, 171–2, **174**, 178, 183–4, 209; *Spiranthes australis* **204**; spotted green tree orchid 172; spotted sun orchid **170**, 171, 172, 177, 183; spurred helmet orchid 32; striped sun orchid 209, **210**, 255; sun orchids 48, 56, 63, 119, 151, 165, 166, **170**, 171, **173**, **174**, 177, 178, 183–4, 209, **210**, 241; swamp sun orchid 209; toothed sun orchid 209; trowel-leaved greenhood orchid 172, **174**, 177; winikā orchid 48, **165**, 172, 177, 195, **196**; winter greenhood orchid 38, 172, **175**, 177, 184, 241
ōrea 39, 151, 166, 187, 199, 211, 247
Oriental Bay 10, 64–8, 71, 73
Ōrongorongo Track (Wainuiomata) 254
Oruaiti Pā 86, **87**
Ōrua-pouanui Baring Head 145, 254
Ōtaki Estuary mouth 255
Ōtari–Wilton's Bush Reserve and Native Botanic Garden 10, 15, 21, 27, **34**, 34–43, 53
Ōtuamotoro Days Bay 10, 145, **164**, 164–76: Wharf 159, 162
Ōwhiro Bay 14, **101**, 106, 107, 114, 121, 123, 127: quarry 99, 117
oystercatchers, South Island pied oystercatcher **154**, 188, 219, 248; variable oystercatcher 95, 99, **103**, 105, 107, **125**, 127, 153, 225, 227, 248

Paehuia ridgeline 52, 53, **55**
Paehuia Ridgeline Track 53, 56
paikea 66, **67**, 106, 129, 156, 244
pakahā 11, 65, 102, 131, 133–4, 155, **159**, 161, 227, 231, 233, 244
pākau 81, 1119, **151**, 241
pākirikiri 99, **101**, 242
panahi 188
pāngurunguru 138–9: (northern giant petrel) **130**; (southern giant petrel) **133**
pānoko (thread fern) **56**
panoko (torrentfish) 247
pāpaka nui 100, **101**
pāpango 187, 240, 248, **251**
pāpapa 166, 168, 184, **185**
papatāniwhaniwha 119
Papatūānuku 34, 86
paradise shelduck 48, 151, 153, 187, 201, **202**, 219, 255
Parangarahu Lakes at Te Rae-akiaki 10, 31, 145, 186–91
paraoā 106, 127, 129, 138–9
Paraparaumu Beach **236**, 241, 244
pārera 187, 250, 250
Pariwhero Red Rocks Scientific Reserve 68, 88, 106, 109, **122**, 122–5, **125**, 126–7
passionfruit, New Zealand 39, 48, **49**, 201
pātangatanga 100, 243
pāteke 11, 25, **26**, 27, 153, 233, 237, 240, 248
pātiki 103, 144
pātōtara 110
pāua: black-foot pāua **101**, 103, 242; silver pāua 103
Pāuatahanui Inlet 219, 227, 228, 240
peka-a-waka 39, 48, **49**, 63, 165, 172, 178, 195
penguin, little blue 9, 11, 14, 22, **65**, **69**, 93, 95, 99, 105, 139, 144, 159, 167, 233, 237, 243
pepe ao uri 123, **252**, 253
pepe para riki 56, 63, 83, **107**, 110, **111**, 121, 123, 151, 162, 241, 253
pepe pōuri 166, **167**, 197, 253
pēpeke nguturoa 42, 166, 168, 197, **210**, 211, 241
pēpepe 63, perch: banded perch 243; butterfly perch 243;

magpie perch 243; sea perch 103
Percy Scenic Reserve and alpine plant collection 15, 145, **200**, 200–5
peripatus, New Zealand 63
petako 56, **57**, 81, 151
Petone Pito One 143, 200: wharf **152**, 153, 155
petrels 129, 138–9: Cape petrel 131, **133**, **136**, 138, 139; common diving petrel 11, 134, 162, **231**; Cook's petrel 134; northern giant petrel **130**, 131, 132; soft-plumaged petrel 131; southern giant petrel 131, 132, **133**; storm petrel 139; Westland petrel 129, 134, 139; white-chinned petrel **131**, 134; white-faced storm petrel 11, 134; white-headed petrel 131
Pharazyn Reserve 255
pigeon, New Zealand 25, **40**, 41, 73, **76**, 93, 110, 147, 166, 255
pigeonwood 41, 181, 195
piharau 199, 247
pīhoihoi 110, **117**, 119, 127, 188, 254
pikirangi 178, **180**, 209
pilchard 65
pinātoro 119, 188, **190**
pines 31, 48, 53, 168, 171, 172
pīngao 97, **100**, 103, 105, 156, **157**, 188
Pinnacles, The **90**, 93
pipit, New Zealand 110, **117**, 119, 127, 188, 254
pīpīwharauroa 36, 39, **57**, 63, 76, 79, 95, 150, 166, 168, 180, 182, 197, 207, 237
piripiri (pygmy tree orchid) 119, **120**
piripiri, sand **95**, 97
Pito One Beach 143, 152–7
Pito One Petone 143, 200: wharf **152**, 153, 155
Pittosporum divaricatum 167
piupiu **195**
pīwakawaka 39, 41, 55, 63, 68, 76, 93, **149**, 150, 161, 166, 168, 181, 211
Places for Penguins project 14, 100
Plimmerton coast **224**, 228, **230**
plover, spur-winged 153, 219, **221**, 227, 248
poaka 153, 188, **219**, 221, 227, 255
pōānanga 113, **181**

pohowera 145, 167, 184, 188, **190**, 191, 219, 221, 248, 254, 255
pōhuehue 103, 123, 156: large-leaved pōhuehue 123
Point Dorset 90
Polhill Protectors Ngā Kaimanaaki o Te Waimapihi 79, 81
Pōneke Wellington waterfront 22, **64**, 64–71
ponga 32, 41, **46**, 53, **54**, 60, 81, 151, 172, 178, 184, 209
pōpokotea 11, 25, **26**, 27, 79, 150, 166, 168, 177, 201, 207, 233, 237, 239, 255
Porirua City Council 14
Porirua Scenic Reserve 254
porokaiwhiri 41, 181, 195
poroporo **53**, 74, 81
Port Nicholson Block Settlement Trust 144, 145
Predator Free 2050 Ltd 110
Predator Free Khandallah 59
Predator Free Miramar 93
Predator Free Mt Vic 74
Predator Free Northland 53
Predator Free Wellington 14
primrose, sea 103, 222, **223**
Princess Bay 101–3
prion, fairy 11, 131, 133, **137**, 231
privet, New Zealand 81, 177, 181
pua o Te Rēinga 42
puapua-a-Autahi 77, 151, 167, 178, 184
puawānanga 68, **70**, 151, 181, 209
puhinui 119, 178, **179**, 203
pukatea 151, 164
pūkeko 151, 187, **220**, 221, 233
Puketahā forest 9, 10, 11, 13, 27, 145, **192**, 192–9, 211
pūkohu 184, 193, 195
pukupuku 76
pūnui 151, 195, 241
pūriri **238**
pūtangitangi 48, 151, 153, 187, 201, **202**, 219, 255
pūwaiwhakarua 103, **104**, 105
pūweto 187, 222, **223**, 254

Queen Elizabeth II Park 255

Radome Track 113
rail, banded **220**, 222

rako 134
RAMBO (Rats and Mustelid Blitzing Ōtari) 53
Rangatira flat 237, 239, 240, 241
Rangatira Loop Track 237
Ranginui 58, 86
rangiora 60, 74, 114, 176, 201
Rangitatau Palmer Head 86, 94–7
Rangituhi Colonial Knob 254
Raoulia australis 114; *R. glabra* 114; *R. hookerii* 123
rapokā 68, **69**, 103, 107, 155, **157**, 228
rātā moehau 39, **40**, 42, 201
rātā vine: scarlet rātā vine 63, 151, 195, 209; white flowering rātā vine 36
rātā: Bartlett's rātā 39, **40**, 42, 201; northern rātā 10, 35, 39, 53, 119, **164**, **170**, 171, 192, 206, 207, **238**, 240, 255
rauhuia 36, 119, **120**
rauparaha 97
raupeka 56, 151, 172, **174**, 177–8, 183
raupō 142, 187, 188, 189, 250
raurenga 60, 151, 172, **175**, 178, 184, 195
rays 9, 10, 64, 102, 105, 156: eagle ray 9, 10, 22, **67**, 68, 71, 228, 243; short-tail stingray 71
Red Rocks Track 113
Remutaka Conservation Trust 14, 193
Remutaka Range 4, 58, 81, 90, 99, 153, 193
Remutaka Saddle Track 255
Remutaka Trig Track 255
reptiles 42, 144, 158, 162; *see* geckos; skinks; tuatara
rereti 46, **47**, 119, 195
rewarewa 36, **37**, 46, 53, 68, 151, 171, 177, 178, 192
Ridge Track 211
rifleman 9, 11, 13, 25, 48, **50**, 55, 79, 166, 168, **169**, 180, 182, 193, 211
rimu 9, 21, 35, **38**, 39, 41, 53, 68, 99, 119, 142, 178, 181, 192, **193**, 206, 207: Moko 21, **38**, 39, 41, 42
rimurapa 91, **92**, 99, 124, 243
rimurimu 89, 99, 105, 184, 228
rimuroa **109**, 110, 178
riroriro 39, 41, 63, 93, 110, 150, 161, 166, 168, **169**, 181, 184, 211

rō 42, 51, 63, 76, **80**, 81, 82, 166
robin, North Island 11, 13, 25, **26**, 27, 32, 79, 150, 233, 237, 240
rocks 124, 207
Rōpū Tiaki 31, 191
Rotary Club of Wellington 74
Roto Kawau 25, 28, 31, 32
Roto Māhanga **24**, 25, 28, 31, 191
Round the Lake Track 31, 32
rowi 11, 199, 231, **232**, 233
ruru 25, **30**, 31, 55, 63, 74, 79, 95, 166, 217, 233, 237, **260**

saddleback 11, 13, 25, **26**, 27, 32, **79**, 199, 216, 237, 240
saltmarsh ribbonwood 95
saltmarshes 218, 222
sand piripiri **95**, 97
sawtail, spotted 243
scabweed, golden *Raoulia australis* 114
scaup, New Zealand 187, 240, 248, **251**
scorpionfish, red 105
sea lions 105
sea stars, reef 100, 243
seabirds 10, 11, 64, 65, 86, 91, 93, 94, 95, 97, 99, 101–2, 105, 107, 127, 128–34, 132–9, 153, 159, 162, 230–1, 233, 244, 247
seahorses 9, 98, **99**, 100, 103, 105
seals 9, 15: Antarctic crabeater seal 103, 105, 155–6; leopard seal 68, **69**, 103, 107, 155, **157**, 228; New Zealand fur seal 9, 10, 65, 91, 94, **97**, 100, 102, **104**, 105, 109, 122, **126**, 129, 155, 161, 228, 243, 244, **245**, 254, **255**; southern elephant seal 68, **70**, 103, 161; subantarctic fur seal 65, **66**, 228; Weddell seal 65, 228
seaweeds 89, 99, 105, 184, 228
sedge, strand 156
shags 10, 11, 32, 93, 102, 107, 155, 222, 254, 255: black shag 187–8, **189**; little black shag 187, **226**, 227; little pied shag 187, 225, **226**, 227; pied shag 32, 225, 227, **229**, 233, 244, **249**, 250; spotted shag 11, **92**, 93, 162, 244
sharks: blue shark 68, 243; carpet shark 228, 243; great white shark 91; rig houndshark 10, 68, **70**, 71, 228; white-spotted dogfish 243
shearwaters 11, 129, 131, 134, 139, 233, 237, **238**: Buller's shearwater 134; fleshfooted shearwater 134; fluttering shearwater 11, 65, 102, 131, 133–4, 155, **159**, 161, 227, 231, 233, 244; short-tailed shearwater 134; sooty shearwater 11, 134, 233, 237, **238**
shelduck, paradise 48, 151, 153, 187, 201, **202**, 219, 255
shellfish 16, 88, 89, 99, 143, 145, 191
shells, marine 156, 184, 228, 253: Arabic volute 228; black-foot pāua shell **101**; common fan scallop shells 184, 228; Cook's turban shell 228; heavy-ribbed venus shell 228; paper nautilus shell 228, 241; pink sunset shell 253; pink top shell 156; pipi shell 253; small toheroa shell 253; spotted tiger topshell 228; top shell 156; tuatua 253; turret shell 228
shoveler, Australasian 187, 240, 248, 250, **251**
silver drummer 243
silvereye 51, 55, 63, 68, 76, **77**, 103, 110, 123, 150, 181
silverspot 243
Silverstream Track 255
Siren Rocks 106, 107: lagoon 106
skinks 11, 31, 42, 158: copper skink 82, 97, 166, 211, 233, 241; glossy brown skink 31, 82, 151, 233; McGregor's skink 11, 233; Newman's speckled skink 233; northern grass skink 36, 82, **97**, 123, 124, 151, 166, 177, 233, **234**, 241; ornate skink **160**, 162, 241; spotted skink 31, **161**, 162, 233
skuas: Arctic skua 134, 159, **160**, 227, 233; south polar skua 131
Skyline Walkway Track 59, 60, 109
slug, sea 105, 127
snails, freshwater 16, 187: *Latia neritoides* 211; *Potamopyrgus oppidanus* 56
snails, land: *Wainuia urnula* 166, 199, 211
snapper 99, 242, 243
snowberry 110: bush snowberry 195
snowdrop wood-sorrel 119, **120**

South Coast Marine Reserve Coalition 99
speargrass 10, 110, 119, **123**
spiders 55, 81: black tunnelweb spider **81**
spinifex 97, 105, 156, 188
spleenworts: shining spleenwort 241; sickle spleenwort 56, **57**, 81, 151
sponges, sea 184, 228, 243
Spooky Gully 88, 113, 116
spoonbill, royal **92**, 93, 153, 219, 227, 240, 250, 254
spotties 243
squid 131: giant squid 129, 138; southern reef squid 100, 105
stick insects 42, 51, 81, 166: brown stick insect **80**; New Zealand giant stick insect 56, 76, 82, 162, 205; prickly stick insect 63; smooth stick insect 76, 80, 82; unarmed stick insect 82
stilt, pied 153, 188, **219**, 221, 227, 255
stingrays *see* rays
stitchbird 9, 11, 13, 25, **26**, 32, 79, 199, 237, **238**, 240
sundew, tall 178, **179**, 180
supplejack 39, 142, 209
swallow, welcome 76, 117, **118**, 187, 218, 222
Swamp Track 25, 27, 31, 32
swan, black 153, 187, 248, **250**

taha pounamu 68, 243
tāiko 129, 134, 139
takahē 11, 13, 25, 28, **29**, 32, 216, 221, 230–1, **235**, 240
takahikare 11, 134
tākapu 65, 93, 102, **138**, 139, 155, 159, **160**, 227
takupurenga 114, 123
tāmure 99, 242, 243
Tāne Mahuta 21, 39
Tangi te Keo 23
Tapu Te Ranga/Taputeranga Island 87, **100**, 105
Taputeranga Marine Reserve and coast 10, 15, 16, 87, **98**, 98–107
tara 10, 11, 65, **70**, 71, 91, 93, 95, 97, 100, 101–2, 131, 134, 139, **152**, 153, 155, 159, **224**, 225, 227, 233, 240, **244**, **246**, 247, 248, 255

Tarakena Bay 86, **94**, 94–7
tarakihi 103
taramea 10, 110, 119, **123**
Taranaki Whānui ki Te Upoko o Te Ika 14, 31, 41, 68, 110, 144, 145, 19, 161, 191, 199
taranui 91, **154**, 155, 247, 254
tarapirohe 95, 97, 101, **102**, 155, 247, 254
tarāpuka 153, **155**, 248, 254
tarāpunga 93, **102**, 105, 107, 127, 131, **152**, 153, 225, 233, 248
Tararua Range 81, 152, 193, 204, 246
tarata 53, **54**, 207, 209
tātarāmoa 41, **60**, 63, 113
tauhinu 63, 99, 123
tauhou 51, 55, 63, 68, 76, **77**, 103, 110, 123, 150, 181
taupata 74, 104
tawa 36, **37**, 41, 60, 99, 119, 151, 178, 192, 201, 240
tawaka 205
tawhai 10, 32, 164, 168, 171, 172, **175**, 176–8, 181, 182, 184, 193, **197**: goblin forest 10, 193, 195, **197**
tāwhirikaro, perching 209
tāwiniwini 110
Te Ahumairangi 22, 27, **52**, 52–5, **55**, 56–7, **64**, 72
Te Ahumairangi Ecological Restoration (TAER) 53
Te Āti Awa 14, 17, 21, 39, 87, 142, 145
Te Awa Kairangi Hutt River 145, 152, 155, 156, 201, **206**, 207, 255: mouth 142, 143, 152–7
Te Awarua-o-Porirua Harbour 219
Te Haape Stream and valley 88, 108, **116**, 116–21, **121**, 123
Te Hoiere pepeketua 11, 31
Te Kopahou Reserve 88, 107, **108**, 108–15, 116, 117, 122: trig 114; visitor centre 116
Te Māhanga Track 25, 32
Te Māra a Tāne 9, 10, 11, 13, 14, 21, 24–33, 42, 48, 53, 55, 59, 73, 78, 79, 82, 110, 191
Te Moana-o-Raukawa Cook Strait 10, 86, 88, 89, 94, 106, 128–31, 133, 138
Te Motu Kairangi – Miramar Ecological Restoration 93
Te Papa Tongarewa Museum of New Zealand 22, 65–6, 68, **71**:

Bush City exhibition 68, **71**;
Te Taiao Nature exhibition 68
Te Rae-akiaki Pencarrow Head 15, 90, **128**, 131, 186–91
Te Raekaihau Point **98**, 99, 101–3, 107
Te Rimurapa Sinclair Head 4, 10, 88, 109, 113, 122–7
Te Taiao Nature exhibition 68
Te Upoko-o-te-Ika 10, 11, 12, 17, 26, 31, 35, 68, 108, 164, 203, 214
Te Whanganui-a-Tara Wellington Harbour 9, 10, 17, 23, 52, 58, 64–6, 68, **72**, **78**, 81, 86, 87, 90, 93, 94, 95, 128, 131, 132, 139, 142–5, 152, 153, 156, 159, 165, 180: entrance 90, 93, 94, 97
teal: black teal 248; brown teal 11, 25, **26**, 27, 153, 233, 237, 240, 248; grey teal 187, **219**
terns 10, 159, 224, 227, 233, 247: Arctic tern 227, 228, 247; black-fronted tern 95, 97, 101, **102**, 134, 155, 225, 247, 254; Caspian tern 91, **154**, 155, 247, 254; eastern little tern 247; Eurasian black tern 225, 247; Eurasian common tern 102, **225**, 247; great crested 247; gull-billed tern 247; sooty tern **225**, 247; white-fronted tern 10, 11, 65, **70**, 71, 91, 93, 95, 97, 100, 101–2, 131, 134, 139, **152**, 153, 155, 159, **224**, 225, 227, 233, 240, **244**, **246**, 247, 248, 255; white-winged black tern 93, 247
Terrace Walk 207
tētē 187, **219**
tī kōuka **13**, 42, 60, 68, 74, 99
tiara 156
tīeke 11, 13, 25, **26**, 27, 32, **79**, 199, 216, 237, 240
Tip Track 113
Tirohanga Track 235
Tītahi Bay 228
titarakura 187, 247
tītī 129: (Cook's petrel) 134; (shearwaters) 11, 129, 131, 134, 139, 233, 237, **238**; (sooty shearwaters) 11, 134, 233, 237, **238**
tītī wainui 11, 131, 133, **137**, 231
titipo 32, **33**, 60
tititipounamu 9, 11, 13, 25, 48, **50**, 55, 79, 166, 168, **169**, 180, 182, 193, 211

titiwai **50**, 51
titoki 46, 53, **54**, 177, 181, 234, 239
toanui 134
toetoe 119, **121**, 187
tohorā 66, **67**, 68, 86, 89, 91, **106**, 129, 244
tohorā puru 99, 106, 124, 129
toitoi 31, 166, 187, 191, 199, 247
tomtit **149**, 150, 168, 177, 182, 193, 197, 207, 255
tōrea 188, **154**, 248
tōrea pango 95, 99, **103**, 105, 107, **125**, 127, 153, 225, 227, 248
toroa 9, 10, 93, 102, **129**, **130**, 131, **132**, 133, **134**, **135**, **136**, 138–9
toropapa, mountain 195
torrentfish 247
tōtara 35, 36, 142
toutouwai 11, 13, 25, **26**, 27, 32, 79, 150, 233, 237, 240
tōwai 36
Transient Track 81
tree daisies 201: coastal tree daisy 114, 123; Gardner's tree daisy 201; heketara tree daisy 201; Kirk's tree daisy 39; rangiora tree daisy 60, 74, 81, 176, 201
tree ferns 9, 36, 48, 166, 255: black tree fern 32, 41, 81, 151, 172, **175**, 184, 201, 209, 241; golden tree fern 209; silver fern 32, 41, **46**, 53, **54**, 60, 81, 151, 172, 178, 184, 209; slender tree fern 151, 195, 241; Smith's tree fern 151; soft tree fern 172, 195, 209, 241
Treehouse 48, 50
trevally 103
Trig Track 237, 240
triplefins 105
trumpeter, striped 105
tuatara 10, 11, 21, **30**, 31, 144, 158, 162
tūī 9, 10, 11, **14**, 25, 35, 36, 41, 44, **45**, 48, 55, 63, 68, 73, 74, 76, 99, 103, 110, 123, 147, 150, 161, 166, 168, 181, 195, 201, 233, **257**
tuna (eels/short-finned eels) 21, 22, 39, 142, 145, 151, 166, 187, 188, 199, 211, 247; *see also* eels; ōrea long-finned eels
turtle, olive ridley 103, 127
tūrutu 171, 178, 207

tussocks 59, 119, 123: silver 105, 114, 123
tutukiwi 32, 48, **49**, 56, 81, 119, 151, 177, **182**, 184, 241
tutumairekurai 156, 244
tūtūmako 110, **114**
tūturiwhatu 221, **247**, 248

Upper Hutt 145, 151, 17, 211, 255
Upper Hutt City Council 14

vegetable sheep 10, 114, 123, 257
violet, mountain 110

waekura 178, 209
waewae kākā 209
Wahlenbergia ramosa 114, **118**, 119
wahu 178, **179**, 180
Waikanae Beach 253
Waikanae Estuary Care Group 14, 253
Waikanae Estuary Scientific Reserve 10, 225, 243, 246–53
Waikanae Jobs for Nature project 253
Waikanae ki Uta ki Tai 253
Waikanae River 247, 253
Waikanae sandspit 15, 16, **246**, 247–8, 253
Waikōkō wetland area 233
Waimanu Lagoon 248, 249, 250, 253
Waimapihi Reserve 23, 27, **78**, 78–83
Wainuiomata Mainland Island 14, 193; *see also* Puketahā Forest
Wainuiomata Old Forest Walk 193
Wainuiomata River 195
Waiotahi Stream 62, 63
Waipapa Loop Track 113
Waipapa Stream 108, 113, 124
Waipiro Bush Walk 46, 48
Waitangi Park wetlands 22, 68, 71
Waiwhetu Stream 142
warbler, grey 39, 41, 63, 93, 110, 150, 161, 166, 168, **169**, 181, 184, 211
warou 76, 117, **118**, 187, 218, 222
Waterfall Bay 243
waterfront, Pōneke Wellington 22, **64**, 64–71
weevils: flax weevil **233**; giraffe weevil 42, 166, 168, 197, **210**, 211, 241; Hutton's speargrass weevil 123, 233

Weir Walk 207
weka 9, 11, 13, 217, 237, **239**, 240
welcome swallow 76, 117, **118**, 187, 218, 222
Wellington Botanic Garden Ki Paekākā 10, 21–2, 27, 44–51, 56
Wellington Botanical Society 234
Wellington City Council (WCC) 14, 21, 28, 46, 53, 77, 81, 100
Wellington Community Trust 110
Wellington Harbour (Te Whanganui-a-Tara) 9, 10, 17, 23, 52, 58, 64–6, 68, **72**, **78**, 81, 86, 87, 90, 93, 94, 95, 128, 131, 132, 139, 142–5, 152, 153, 156, 159, 165, 180: entrance 90, 93, 94, 97
werewere-kōkako 167, 178
wētā 166, 217: cave wētā 31, 82, 151, 205; Cook Strait giant wētā 9, 11, 31, 81, 82, **83**, 158, 162, 199, 233; ground wētā 63, 197; Wellington tree wētā 31, 51, 56, 63, 76, **81**, 82, 162, 168, 233
weweia **187**, 250, 254, 255
whai 71
whai keo 9, 10, 22, **67**, 68, 71, 228, 243
Whairepo Lagoon 10, 22, 65, 68
whakahao 105
Whakahoua 243
Whale and Dolphin Watch – Wellington Facebook group 12, 68
whales 16, 91, 106, 129, 159: blue whale 99, 106, 124, 127, 129; humpback whale 66, **67**, 106, 127, 129, 156, 244; killer whale *see* maki orca; pygmy right whale 106, 156; pygmy sperm whale 106; southern right whale 66, **67**, 68, 86, 89, 91, 103, 105, **106**, 129, 244, 254; sperm whale 106, 127, 129, 138–9
whales, beaked 106, 127, 228: Arnoux's beaked whale 106, 228; Shepherd's beaked whale 127, 228
wharangi 53
wharariki **14**, 25, **94**, 95, 99, 103, 105, 114, 123, 156, 234
Whare Mahana 144
wharengārara 151
Whātaitai 23, 87
whau 36
whauwhaupaku 31, 53,181, 240

whē 121, 162, **163**
wheke 88, 99, 100, 103, **104**, 105, 243
wheke nui 129, 138
wheki 60, 151, 195, 209
wheki-ponga 209
whitehead 11, 25, **26**, 27, 79, 150, 166, 168, 177, 201, 207, 233, 237, 239, 255
whiteywood 25, 53, 60, 74, 81, 114, 123, 176, 181, 201, 234, 240
Whitireia Park Reserve 224
wī 105, 114, 123
Wild Plants of Wellington 12
Wilkinson Track 236–41
Williams Park 168, 176
wineberry **59**, 60
winikā 48, **165**, 172, 177, 195, **196**, 197
wood rose 42
woollyhead **109**, 110
worm, velvet 63
wrasses: banded wrasse 103, 243; scarlet wrasse 103, **104**, 105
wrybill 248

yellow-eye mullet 65

Zealandia Te Māra a Tāne 9, 10, 11, 13, 14, 21, **24**, 24–33, 42, 48, 53, 55, 59, 73, 78, 79, 82, 110, 191

Michael Szabo and Te Papa Press are grateful for generous funding from the
Te Papa Foundation, which has enabled us to send a copy to each school in
Te Upoko-o-te-Ika, and to the Deane Endowment Trust for their continued support.

First published in New Zealand in 2024 by
Te Papa Press, PO Box 467, Wellington, New Zealand
www.tepapapress.co.nz

Text © Michael Szabo
Mana whenua contributions © as credited, except pages 215–217, which is
adapted from an article by Lee-Anne Duncan originally published in the
January/February 2019 issue of *NZ Life & Leisure*.
Images © as credited on page 261.

This book is copyright. Apart from any fair dealing for the purpose of private
study, research, criticism, or review, as permitted under the Copyright Act, no
part of this book may be reproduced by any process, stored in a retrieval system,
or transmitted in any form, without the prior permission of the Museum of
New Zealand Te Papa Tongarewa.

TE PAPA® is the trademark of the Museum of New Zealand Te Papa Tongarewa
Te Papa Press is an imprint of the Museum of New Zealand Te Papa Tongarewa

A catalogue record is available from the National Library of New Zealand

ISBN 978-1-99-116557-2

Design by Floor van Lierop (thisisthem.com)
Cover illustration and maps by Angela Keoghan, The Picture Garden
Digital imaging by Jeremy Glyde
Printed by 1010 Printing International Limited, China